SAGE PUBLISHING: OUR STORY

We believe in creating fresh, cutting-edge content that helps you prepare your students to make an impact in today's ever-changing business world. Founded in 1965 by 24-year-old entrepreneur Sara Miller McCune, SAGE continues its legacy of equipping instructors with the tools and resources necessary to develop the next generation of business leaders.

- We invest in the right **authors** who distill the best available research into practical applications.

- We offer intuitive **digital solutions** at student-friendly prices.

- We remain permanently independent and fiercely committed to **quality, innovation, and learning.**

Leadership
Case Studies in Education

Second Edition

To the profession of teaching and the special teachers within the profession who guided me and gave me the opportunity to succeed.

—Peter G. Northouse

For all those souls who endeavor to be educators.

—Marie Lee

Sara Miller McCune founded SAGE Publishing in 1965 to support the dissemination of usable knowledge and educate a global community. SAGE publishes more than 1000 journals and over 800 new books each year, spanning a wide range of subject areas. Our growing selection of library products includes archives, data, case studies and video. SAGE remains majority owned by our founder and after her lifetime will become owned by a charitable trust that secures the company's continued independence.

Los Angeles | London | New Delhi | Singapore | Washington DC | Melbourne

Leadership
Case Studies in Education

Second Edition

Peter G. Northouse

Marie Lee

Los Angeles | London | New Delhi
Singapore | Washington DC | Melbourne

FOR INFORMATION:

SAGE Publications, Inc.
2455 Teller Road
Thousand Oaks, California 91320
E-mail: order@sagepub.com

SAGE Publications Ltd.
1 Oliver's Yard
55 City Road
London EC1Y 1SP
United Kingdom

SAGE Publications India Pvt. Ltd.
B 1/I 1 Mohan Cooperative Industrial Area
Mathura Road, New Delhi 110 044
India

SAGE Publications Asia-Pacific Pte. Ltd.
3 Church Street
#10–04 Samsung Hub
Singapore 049483

Acquisitions Editor: Maggie Stanley
Content Development Editor: Lauren Holmes
Editorial Assistant: Alissa Nance
Production Editor: Bennie Clark Allen
Copy Editor: Melinda Masson
Typesetter: C&M Digitals (P) Ltd.
Proofreader: Jennifer Grubba
Indexer: Mary Mortensen
Cover Designer: Gail Buschman
Marketing Manager: Amy Lammers

Printed in the United States of America

Library of Congress Cataloging-in-Publication Data

Names: Northouse, Peter Guy, author. | Lee, Marie (Journalist), author.

Title: Leadership case studies in education / Peter G. Northouse, Western Michigan University, Marie Lee.

Description: Second Edition. | Los Angeles : SAGE, [2018] | Includes bibliographical references and index.

Identifiers: LCCN 2017049582 | ISBN 9781544310428 (Paperback : acid-free paper)

Subjects: LCSH: Leadership—Case studies. | Educational leadership.

Classification: LCC LB2806 .N64 2018 | DDC 371.2—dc23 LC record available at https://lccn.loc.gov/2017049582

This book is printed on acid-free paper.

18 19 20 21 22 10 9 8 7 6 5 4 3 2 1

Brief Contents

Detailed Contents

Preface

This book looks at leadership through the eyes of educators. From university presidents and district superintendents to those who teach or sit in the classroom, education is a discipline that has leadership at its very core.

Leadership Case Studies in Education (2nd ed.) is designed as a companion text to Northouse's *Leadership: Theory and Practice* (8th ed.), which is one of the best-selling textbooks on leadership in the world. Over the years, those in the disciplines of education and educational leadership have become one of the textbook's largest audiences, with the book being used in courses from undergraduate teacher training to graduate studies. It is clear, however, that education presents a set of variables and issues that are not universally shared in the wider world of leadership. In recognition of this, and in response to many requests that we do so, we developed *Leadership Case Studies in Education* (2nd ed.) to provide field-specific case studies for educators and those who teach them.

To create *Leadership Case Studies in Education* (2nd ed.), we sought out educators at many levels to provide us with real case scenarios from their experiences. We have many named contributors in the text who have authored thought-provoking and intriguing cases. For other cases, educators participated in interviews and provided background that allowed the authors to construct studies from that information. All cases are from real life—they are true stories of situations encountered by educators whether it is the head of a school who is reluctant to use or implement technology or a professor who must deal with subtle racism and elitism experienced by a student in her class.

SPECIAL FEATURES

Leadership Case Studies in Education (2nd ed.) follows the chapter content established in Northouse's *Leadership: Theory and Practice* (8th ed.) and employs Northouse's same clear, concise, and informative approach. In addition, several other features of *Leadership Case Studies in Education* (2nd ed.) help make the book user-friendly for the education field:

- Each chapter begins with a short narrative describing the leadership approach being addressed in the corresponding chapter of *Leadership: Theory and Practice* (8th ed.). This narrative is not designed to be inclusive of all the concepts discussed in the corresponding chapter, but provides enough information to remind the reader of some key concepts.

- Each chapter has two case studies: one for the pre-K–12 segment of the education discipline and one for the higher education segment.

- Questions at the end of the case studies have been designated as "Questions" and "Advanced Questions." Questions can be answered from the basic synopsis provided in the narrative and are designed for those who may be using *Leadership Case Studies in Education* (2nd ed.) as a supplemental text for courses in education at the undergraduate or graduate level. Advanced Questions require a broader understanding of the concepts and approaches as provided in *Leadership: Theory and Practice* (8th ed.) and are designed for students who are simultaneously reading, or who have read, that companion book.

- Figures and tables are provided within the narrative to illustrate key concepts.

- Chapter 15 on gender and leadership provides in-depth and up-to-date information and data on women in the education field to help stimulate reflection and discussion.

- New to this edition (and in *Leadership: Theory and Practice*, 8th ed.) is a chapter that addresses followership, an emerging leadership concept that is the reversal of the leader-centric perspective of other approaches.

- This edition also features case studies for the psychodynamic approach to leadership, which appeared in recent editions of *Leadership: Theory and Practice* but is not in the eighth edition. We recognize that many educators may still want to study this theory of leadership, and so content for the psychodynamic approach is available online (see **study.sagepub.com/ northouselee2e**).

Through these special features, every effort has been made to make *Leadership Case Studies in Education* (2nd ed.) a substantive and applicable text for those studying leadership in education.

AUDIENCE

Leadership Case Studies in Education (2nd ed.) provides a discussion of leadership theory and how it applies to real-life situations in all levels of the educational discipline. Thus, it is intended for undergraduate and graduate classes in education and educational leadership.

This book can also be used as a supplemental text for courses in education at the undergraduate and graduate levels. Specifically, it is well suited for classes in educational leadership, leadership in higher education, school leadership, curriculum design, instructional supervision, adult education, staff development, learning theory, principalship, educational foundations, assessment, and educational administration. *Leadership Case Studies in Education* (2nd ed.) would also be useful as a text in continuing education, in-service training, and professional development programs for educators and those working in the education field.

ACKNOWLEDGMENTS

The authors would like to express their appreciation to the many individuals who directly or indirectly played a role in the development of this book. First, we would like to thank the many people at SAGE Publishing, in particular, our editor Maggie Stanley, who has been instrumental in making the concept become a printed reality. In addition, we would like to thank production editor Bennie Clark Allen and copy editor Melinda Masson.

For their input on the concept and manuscript in its initial stages and comprehensive reviews of the manuscript, we would like to thank the following reviewers:

Edward E. Ackerley, *Northern Arizona University*

Nathan Alleman, *Baylor University*

Katya Armistead, *University of California, Santa Barbara*

Prince Attoh, *University of Maryland Eastern Shore*

Murat Baglibel, *Gaziantep Üniversitesi*

Don Beaudette, *Boston University*

Bonnie M. Beyer, *University of Michigan-Dearborn*

Jim Bird, *University of North Carolina at Charlotte*

Marilyn Bugenhagen, *Marian University*

Roger Buskill, *University of Louisville*

Kathy Campbell, *Southeastern Louisiana University*

Jan Carlson, *Oklahoma State University*

Sharon Carter, *Davidson County Community College*

Steven F. Cheeseman, *Fordham University*

Cynthia M. Compton, *Wingate University*

Ron Cugno, *Nova Southeastern University*

Mark D'Amico, *University of North Carolina at Charlotte*

Gary Dean, *Indiana University of Pennsylvania*

David De Jong, *University of South Dakota*

Paul W. Decker, *Woodbury University*

Alaster Scott Douglas, *University of Roehampton*

Chastity W. English, *North Carolina A&T State University*

Walter Enloe, *Hamline University*

Priva Fischweicher, *Barry University*

Margie Flores-Vance, *Drury University*

John Freeman, *University of Tennessee at Chattanooga*

David Freitas, *Indiana University South Bend*
Maria Gallo, *St. Angela's College*
Amy Garrett Dikkers, *University of North Carolina Wilmington*
Manny Gomez, *Wright University*
John E. Gray, *Stockton University*
Kathy Guthrie, *Florida State University*
John Hardman, *Florida Atlantic University*
Deborah Harley-McClaskey, *East Tennessee State University*
Meta Harris, *Baltimore City Community College*
Sunil Hazari, *University of West Georgia*
Trace Hebert, *Lipscomb University*
Kate Hudson, *University of Massachusetts Amherst*
Christine M. Imbra, *St. Cloud State University*
Stephanie J. Jones, *Texas Tech University*
Sheila Joyner, *Sam Houston State University*
Eric Kaufman, *Virginia Tech*
Patricia Kelly-Stiles, *Fordham University*
Steve Laing, *Utah State University*
E. Wayne Lord, *Georgia Regents University*
Heather Maietta, *Regis College*
Janice Maitland, *Caribbean Union College*
John McKay, *Wingate University*
Roxanne M. Mitchell, *University of Alabama*
Joseph Mukuni, *Virginia Tech University*
Benjamin C. Ngwudike, *Jackson State University*
Frances O'Reilly, *University of Montana*
Anita Pankake, *University of Nebraska–Lincoln*
Paola Pedrelli, *Birmingham City University*
Lou Sabina, *Stetson University*
Alan Sebel, *Touro College*
Kaye Shelton, *Lamar University*
Ron Siers Jr., *Salisbury University*
David Stader, *Southeast Missouri State University*
Thomas J. Starmack, *Bloomsburg University*
Jo Swain, *Rocky Mountain College*
Renee Wallace, *Florida Agriculture and Mechanical University*

Cynthia Ward, *Johnson & Wales University*
Karen Wetherill, *University of North Carolina Wilmington*
Jennifer Williams Molock, *University of Utah*
Nancy Wolf, *Lesley University*

Critiques by these reviewers were invaluable in helping to focus our thinking and fine-tune the case studies and text.

INSTRUCTOR RESOURCES

For teaching notes to accompany the cases in this book, visit the instructor resource site at **study.sagepub.com/northouselee2e**. The teaching notes include case summaries, analyses, and answers to the cases' questions.

1

Introduction

INTRODUCTION

There are few professions that one can say are synonymous with leadership. Education is one of those. By the very nature of what educators choose to do—facilitate the teaching of others—they are leaders.

Leadership is a complex phenomenon that has many definitions and is conceptualized in a variety of ways. How one approaches leadership is based on many things, from your cultural orientation and experiences to your personal beliefs, attitudes, and values.

Despite the multitude of ways in which leadership has been conceptualized, the following components are identified as central to the phenomenon: (a) Leadership is a process, (b) leadership involves influence, (c) leadership occurs in groups, and (d) leadership involves common goals. Based on these components, the following definition of leadership is used in this text:

> *Leadership* is a process whereby an individual influences a group of individuals to achieve a common goal.

1

Following this definition, it is easy to see why education and leadership seem to go hand in hand. Whether one is in the classroom or the administration building, in front of students or facilitating school admissions, individuals in the discipline of education are influencing others to achieve a common goal. That common goal is to create a safe place where students can effectively learn and grow.

That is why the study of leadership is particularly salient to the field of education. In this book *we examine how leadership theories can be applied specifically to educational settings.* The leadership theories we discuss can be as simple as the trait approach, where leadership is defined by characteristics leaders possess, to more contemporary approaches such as adaptive leadership, which looks at how leaders guide followers through change, or followership, which examines the role followers play in leadership.

The field of leadership has grown exponentially in the last two decades, and there are many established leadership theories, each of which conceptualizes leadership from a unique perspective. However, the discipline of educational leadership has often addressed leadership with an emphasis on administration, curriculum, and instruction, giving less attention to leadership theory. As a result, there is a large, untapped body of information on leadership theory that can assist educators in understanding the dynamics of leadership in education.

The need for leadership in education is unprecedented. Research studies show that talented leadership plays a pivotal role in improving student achievement (Miller, 2015). Clearly, it is incumbent on the profession of education to pay close attention to developing leaders by making sure they get the proper training.

To better understand how select leadership theories have value in educational settings, it is worthwhile to discuss these approaches using authentic case examples. As Bush (2011) has pointed out, the relevance of theory to good practice as an educator is that theories and concepts can provide a framework for leaders' decision making as well as provide a rationale for those decisions. This is important because many educators "mistakenly rely mainly upon experience and intuition—with all the limitations to change which these contain—to guide them through their careers" (Day, 2003, p. 46). Admittedly, many people struggle with connecting theoretical concepts with the practice. The case study approach taken in this book is an attempt to close this gap.

In the research literature, there exists a deficit of articles that address how leadership theories can be applied to an examination of leadership in pre-K–12 and higher education settings. One exception is the work of Bess and Goldman (2001), which explores the utility of five leadership theories (situational, charismatic, transformational, path–goal, and leader–member exchange [LMX]) in explaining leader behavior in K–12 schools and university settings. They point out that the leadership challenges faced by educators in these settings are affected by distinct modes of authority, the nature of everyday work, professional norms and assumptions, and the general dispositions of the educators who work in these settings.

Some leadership concepts work better in one setting than another. For example, Bess and Goldman (2001) argue that charismatic leadership is unhelpful as an explanation of leadership effectiveness in universities but valuable as it applies to K–12 schools that are less privileged where charismatic leadership has been used as an antidote to discouragement and disengagement, providing inspiration and hope to teachers and students alike.

One of the best ways to apply and understand theoretical concepts is through the experiential learning rooted in the use of case studies. Cases are detailed, narrative accounts of situations that have been encountered in a chosen field. Employing case studies has been shown to encourage critical thinking (Popil, 2011), a finding echoed by Youngblood and Beitz (2001) who reported that experiential learning strategies, like the analysis and discussion of case studies, promote the development of critical thinking skills in individuals. In addition, case studies provide an avenue for using problem-solving skills and promote decision making in a nonthreatening environment (Popil, 2011).

That is the goal behind *Leadership Case Studies in Education* (2nd ed.). Designed to be a companion book to Northouse's *Leadership: Theory and Practice* (8th ed.), *Case Studies in Education* provides case studies tailored for those studying education and educational leadership.

The leadership theories and approaches discussed in *Leadership: Theory and Practice* (8th ed.) can be universally applied to many disciplines and organizations. Using cases directly from educational settings will help you to understand the leadership aspects of being an educator. For example, one case in this book analyzes an elementary teacher in terms of her leadership traits and how they play into her teaching situation. In another chapter, a case describes a university president's leadership style and how it hindered her from being as effective as she could have been. In both of these examples, the concepts from the chapter in the theory book help to explore, explain, and solve the dilemmas facing the educators.

The cases in this book are written by a number of contributors and practitioners from many levels—from teachers to administrators—and reflect issues and situations that have actually occurred. The cases directly correspond to the leadership approaches and concepts in *Leadership: Theory and Practice* (8th ed.), and there are two cases for each approach: one for those focused on pre-K–12 education and one for those studying leadership in higher education.

Case studies are an active learning method: They do not give simple answers; rather, they provoke students to employ critical thinking skills to apply the use of theoretical concepts to practical problems (Dowd & Davidhizar, 1999). A critical part of using case studies as a teaching strategy is the discussion that cases can invoke. Research by Levin (1995) shows that case discussion is especially valuable to students and beginning teachers because it leads to clearer understandings of the issues presented in the cases, as well as providing a catalyst for recognizing the need to change one's own thinking.

Our book is intended to help teachers and administrators understand leadership theory and to be able to apply this understanding to their own practice. The format we use in the book is the same for each chapter. We begin each chapter with a basic introduction of a leadership approach or theory that is described in more detail in *Leadership: Theory and Practice* (8th ed.). The reader will then find two cases— one written from a pre-K–12 perspective and a second from the higher education perspective. Each of these levels of the education discipline has unique qualities and challenges, and the cases seek to reflect the different variables educators face in both arenas. Following the cases are questions that will help readers to apply the concepts to the situations. The questions often ask the readers to reflect on what they would do or how they would approach the situation outlined in the case.

You can start with the case study approach here: The following two case studies provide a look at leadership from the macro level, but with many of the nuances that are encompassed in the approaches explored in *Leadership: Theory and Practice* (8th ed.). These are not cases that you can answer quickly, but are reflective of the kind of leadership issues that educators face every day.

CASE STUDIES

The following case studies illustrate the role of leadership in decision making in educational settings. The first case looks at an elementary school principal trying to place students with special needs equitably among his teachers. The second case explores a university president's decision to implement a new college over the objections of the board that governs her.

At the end of each case, you will find two sets of questions that will help in analyzing the case. The first set can be answered using information provided in this chapter; the second set, Advanced Questions, provides an opportunity for deeper exploration of the definition and evolution of leadership and is designed to coincide with the concepts discussed in Chapter 1 of *Leadership: Theory and Practice* (8th ed., pp. 1–18).

CASE 1.1

BALANCING THE WORKLOAD

After getting the new student rosters from the district, Northwest Elementary School's principal, Xavier Morgan, has asked to meet with his three third-grade teachers. Northwest is in a public school district that employs Schools of Choice so that parents can request their children go to any district school even if it isn't their neighborhood school. Northwest is considered the best elementary in the city, so parents whose children struggle with dyslexia, autism spectrum disorder, ADHD, ADD, and other behavioral and learning disabilities are increasingly requesting that their children be enrolled at Northwest. There are 14 new students coming to Northwest Elementary in the third-grade class, and 10 of them are considered special needs.

Every spring, the third-grade teachers meet with the second-grade teachers to discuss the children moving up from the second grade, what their strengths and challenges are, and what type of class environment is best for them. The teachers spend a long time and a great deal of consideration in placing the students—balancing out gender, achievement, attitude, and behavior. They've been known to separate best friends and pair up socially awkward kids so that the social and behavioral environment is balanced as well.

There is no doubt that the new students with special needs will require extra time and patience from their teachers. Children's behavioral issues can adversely affect the learning environment of an entire classroom. While all the third-grade teachers have had professional development training in teaching kids with special needs, Mr. Morgan knows that not all of them are ideally suited to working with impacted children.

One teacher in particular, Mr. Terrell, has a hard time managing the students who need extra instruction, whether he is accommodating or redirecting them in order to give them an optimum learning environment. Mr. Terrell, who has taught at Northwest for 17 years, does an outstanding job with advanced students but begrudgingly adheres to and attends 504 meetings and IEP meetings for students. Parents have complained to Mr. Morgan that Mr. Terrell is indifferent to their children's special needs and resistant to working with them to improve the situation. The school's inclusion teacher and the teacher consultant have told Mr. Morgan that Mr. Terrell is the most difficult teacher on staff to work with. Mr. Morgan, however, believes that it is important for Mr. Terrell's professional development that he continue to learn and improve his skills in this area.

Mr. Morgan knows that the newest third-grade teacher, Mrs. Rodriguez, who has been teaching for only five years, is excellent at working with children with special needs. She devoted her master's degree work to alternative learning initiatives for kids with special needs and has presented at statewide teachers' conferences on a new handwriting program for kids who struggle with dyspraxia and dysgraphia. She also convinced Mr. Morgan to drop plans to teach cursive writing to the third graders, using that time instead to fine-tune the students' printed writing and learn keyboarding. Mrs. Rodriguez is also pregnant and will be taking maternity leave for the rest of the school year after her baby is born in February.

Mrs. D'Amelio, a 10-year teaching veteran, is also good with special needs students. This past year she had two boys in her class who were on the autism spectrum. Their behavioral issues often disrupted the classroom to the point where the boys spent at least an hour each day with Mr. Morgan or in the school psychologist's office completing their classwork. Mrs. D'Amelio spent many hours outside of her class meeting the boys' parents and therapists to develop methods and tools to work with the boys. Then, in March, one of Mrs. D'Amelio's female students died in a car accident, and it had a great emotional impact on the teaching veteran. Mr. Morgan had hoped to give Mrs. D'Amelio a less impacted class to manage this year to allow her to get her bearings back.

(Continued)

(Continued)

In his meeting with the teachers, Mr. Morgan gives them a document outlining the new students and their special needs and accommodations. "We have 14 new students this year, and 10 of them are going to require our very best teaching skills," he says. "I know you have spent a lot of time creating your class rosters, and I am asking you for your participation in placing these students so that we maintain the careful consideration that went into creating your class environments."

The teachers spend a long moment looking over the list. After they've had several minutes, Mr. Morgan starts with Mr. Terrell. "Steve, which of these students would best fit into your current classroom? How many would you be willing to take?"

Mr. Terrell pauses for a long time and then pushes the list away, obviously upset. "Xavier, this is ridiculous!" he says. "We spent hours last spring getting our rosters rounded out, and now you're making us choose these kids like we're picking teams for kickball. We don't know anything about these students other than what's written on this paper. There's no way to know whose class they belong in. It is unfair that you put this on us. You're the boss, you have the PhD, so why don't you assign them to the classes?"

After a tense, quiet moment, Mr. Morgan answers. "I don't want to do that, Steve, because that's not the kind of leader I want to be.

"And Steve," he adds, "it's not the kind of leadership I would hope from my teachers either."

Questions

1. Using the definition of leadership identified above, would you say Mr. Morgan and his teachers have a common goal? What is that goal?

2. Who are the leaders in this situation, and who are the followers? What components of the leadership definition did you use to determine that?

3. In this situation, Mr. Terrell is challenging the principal's leadership. If you were Mr. Morgan, the principal, how would you respond to this challenge?

Advanced Questions

4. Is Mr. Morgan a manager or a leader? How about each of his three third-grade teachers?

5. What type and bases of power do you think Mr. Morgan has? Which of these is he exercising in this situation?

6. If you were Mr. Morgan, how would you proceed in getting the goal achieved?

—*Authors*

CASE 1.2

PRESIDENT SEVERS, YOU'RE FIRED

When Yolanda Severs was fired as the president of Broder State University, it was a dismissal that many of the faculty who served under her said she should have seen coming. But a larger contingent of the campus and the community the university is located in responded with outrage. What did she do that was so bad? She started an engineering college.

Broder State University is one of five state universities or colleges in a sparsely populated western state. The State Board of Higher Education, a politically appointed committee of 12 men and women, administers all five of the higher education institutions in the state, doling out funding and overseeing curriculum and program and degree offerings at the institutions. They also hire and fire the presidents at the universities.

The state has two dominant universities; both are Tier 1 research universities, and the State Board has evenly divided the choice programs between them. One school is considered the law, engineering, and science university; the other is the medical and liberal arts university. Members of the State Board are predominantly alumni from those two universities, and they regard Broder State as the black sheep of the state university system. Unlike the other two universities, which are both more than a century old, Broder didn't become a university until the 1970s, after serving as a junior college for 30 years. Broder's primary programs are education, business, and information technology.

Broder is located in Springville, a town that has experienced explosive growth. The impetus for the growth comes from the technology companies that call Springville home. Bridger Technologies, a very large international software company started by two Broder graduates, employs 10,000 people in Springville alone. Additional companies, many based in technology and engineering, have chosen to locate in Springville. Because of the abundance of jobs and affordable cost of living, the town's population has quadrupled since Broder became a university.

Broder State University has also enjoyed a healthy expansion in its enrollment, and as a result, the State Board of Higher Education has had to channel more funding into the university to meet the growing demands. Enrollment at the other state universities has fallen with many students choosing to go to Broder for general education courses because it is more affordable and in an exciting, growing metropolitan area.

The founders of Bridger Technologies, along with several of the CEOs of other local companies, formed a group called the Technology Consortium and asked Severs to be a member. She soon found out why: The companies were having a hard time getting skilled workers and believed one reason was because Broder didn't offer the necessary programs to provide students with the skills needed to work in the city's companies. The consortium asserted that Broder needed an engineering school that would train design engineers, industrial engineers, software engineers, mechanical engineers, and electrical engineers—all skills needed by the local industry.

Severs agreed and assigned the school's provost and the dean of the College of Arts and Sciences to work with the consortium to put together a curriculum proposal, which she and the two Bridger founders presented to the State Board. They made their case clear: Broder wasn't meeting the needs of its own community with its current academic offerings. "We're outdated," Severs stated. "We have to offer the programs our students need to get the education required to be able to work and live in Springville."

The State Board quickly rejected the proposal, saying, "The state already has an engineering school." Severs pointed out that the engineering school at the other state university was 12 hours from

(Continued)

Springville and didn't offer specialized engineering programs in collaboration with local industry. Broder State's proposed program would offer students abundant internships and co-op working opportunities that would augment their education. The State Board still said no.

The Technology Consortium was undaunted. They came back to Severs with a new plan: They would provide $50 million in private funding to start a School of Engineering at Broder State. The consortium would also pay for a public relations advocacy firm to create public awareness and support for the school. And, the icing on the cake: The state's newly elected governor had pledged his support and vowed to put pressure on the State Board of Higher Education to approve the school.

Things moved with lightning speed. The gift was announced, and the State Board of Higher Education publicly responded that it would not approve the project. The advocacy campaign kicked in, the public demanded the State Board approve the plan, the governor put pressure on the State Board, and within a year Broder's new School of Engineering was under construction. It opened 18 months later with its first class of students. As a result, Broder's enrollment spiked again, outpacing the other two state universities.

The opening of the School of Engineering coincided with Severs's employment review with the State Board. At the beginning of the meeting, the Board's chairman read the following statement from Severs's contract: "The president of Broder State University serves at the pleasure of the State Board of Higher Education." He went on to say that, after a review of Severs's performance, the State Board no longer had confidence in her ability to serve as president of Broder State University. The Board voted unanimously to fire Yolanda Severs.

Despite the outrage that followed, Severs was not reinstated. In interview after interview, Severs maintained that she did what was best for Broder State University. Those who were in favor of the State Board of Higher Education's move said that she overstepped her bounds as a leader and was "empire-building." The governor even spoke out in favor of Severs. All to no avail.

Six months after she was fired, Severs was hired to run a university in a neighboring state.

Questions

1. Who are the leaders in this situation, and who are the followers? What components of the leadership definition did you use to determine that?

2. Leadership occurs in groups. Identify the various groups in this situation and how their leaders used influence within those groups.

3. Leadership is about advancing the common good. What common good was the State Board advocating for? What about Dr. Severs?

Advanced Questions

4. What types of power were exhibited by the leaders in this case? Explain your answer.

5. Does Severs exhibit process or trait leadership?

6. Although she was assigned to be the leader, Severs tried to emerge as the real leader at Broder State University. In what ways did she fail, and why?

—Authors

REFERENCES

Bess, J. L., & Goldman, P. (2001). Leadership ambiguity in universities and K–12 schools and the limits of contemporary leadership theory. *Leadership Quarterly, 12*(4), 419–450.

Bush, T. (2011). *Theories of educational leadership and management* (4th ed.). Thousand Oaks, CA: SAGE.

Day, C. (2003). The changing learning needs of heads: Building and sustaining effectiveness. In A. Harris, C. Day, D. Hopkins, M. Hadfield, A. Hargreaves, & C. Chapman (Eds.), *Effective leadership for school improvement* (pp. 26–52). London, UK: RoutledgeFalmer.

Dowd, S. B., & Davidhizar, R. (1999). Using case studies to teach clinical problem solving. *Nurse Educator, 24*(5), 42–46.

Levin, B. B. (1995). Using the case method in teacher education: The role of discussion and experience in teachers' thinking about cases. *Teaching & Teacher Education, 12*(1), 63–79.

Miller, W. (2015, April 17). Want reform? Principals matter, too. *New York Times*. Retrieved from www.nytimes.com

Popil, I. (2011). Promotion of critical thinking by using case studies as teaching method. *Nurse Education Today, 31*, 204–207.

Youngblood, N., & Beitz, J. M. (2001). Developing critical thinking with active learning strategies. *Nurse Educator, 26*, 39–42.

2

Trait Approach

INTRODUCTION

If you ever say someone has "what it takes" to be a leader or is "born to be a leader," you are describing the underlying premise that has driven much of the research on the trait approach to leadership.

The trait approach has its roots in leadership theory that suggests that certain people are born with special traits that make them great leaders. The trait approach is concerned with what traits leaders exhibit and who has these traits. It is an approach that focuses exclusively on the leader, not on the followers or the situation.

From the multitude of studies conducted through the years on personal characteristics, it is clear that many traits do contribute to leadership. Some of the important traits that are consistently identified in many of these studies are intelligence, self-confidence, determination, integrity, and sociability (Table 2.1). In addition, researchers have found a strong relationship between leadership and the traits described by the *five-factor personality model. Extraversion* was the trait most strongly associated

Table 2.1 Major Leadership Traits

- Intelligence
- Self-confidence
- Determination

- Integrity
- Sociability

SOURCE: Adapted from Northouse, P. G. (2019). *Leadership theory and practice* (8th ed.). Thousand Oaks, CA: SAGE. Adapted with permission.

with leadership, followed by *conscientiousness*, *openness*, *low neuroticism*, and *agreeableness*.

Very closely related to the trait approach is the more contemporary research emphasis on strengths and leadership. The idea behind strengths leadership is that individuals have talents at which they excel or thrive. From these talents, strengths emerge. Strengths leadership requires leaders to recognize and capitalize on not only their own strengths but those of their followers as well.

The trait approach suggests that schools will work better if the people in positions of authority have designated leadership profiles. In choosing principals, administrators, and other leaders, a candidate's traits play a huge role in the selection process. To find the right people, it is common for organizations to use trait assessment instruments. The assumption behind these procedures is that selecting the right people will increase organizational effectiveness. Following this model, schools can specify the characteristics or traits that are important to them for particular positions and then use trait assessment measures to determine whether an individual fits their needs.

The trait approach is also used for personal awareness and development. By analyzing their own traits, individuals can learn their strengths and weaknesses, and get a feel for how others in the organization see them. A trait assessment gives individuals a clearer picture of who they are as leaders and how they fit into the organizational hierarchy. In areas where their traits are lacking, leaders can try to make changes in what they do or where they work to increase their traits' potential impact.

CASE STUDIES

The following case studies illustrate how the trait approach can be applied to leadership in educational settings. The first case looks at a middle school principal who must select a new assistant principal from two qualified candidates. The second case examines why a university administrator is not being considered for a promotion.

At the end of each case, you will find two sets of questions that will help in analyzing the case. The first set can be answered using information provided in this chapter; the second set, Advanced Questions, provides an opportunity for deeper exploration of the trait approach to leadership and is designed to coincide with the concepts discussed in Chapter 2 of *Leadership: Theory and Practice* (8th ed., pp. 19–42).

CASE 2.1

HIRING A NEW ASSISTANT MIDDLE SCHOOL PRINCIPAL

An affluent public school district in the Midwest is completing construction on a new middle school housing students in Grades 6–8. The school is slated to open in the fall, and the district administrative team has filled all the building's leadership positions except for the assistant principal. The role of assistant principal includes managing school operations, discipline, parent conferences, and instruction planning.

Maureen Moser, a dynamic, engaging, intelligent leader with eight years of building-level administrative experience, is being transferred to the new building as its lead principal. She has a reputation for being confident, determined, and sociable with all members of the staff and community. Maureen assembled a team of five individuals comprising teachers, support staff, and parents to assist her in selecting the new assistant principal.

Most of the applications received are from certified administrators with no administrative experience. After two months of screening applications, the team has interviewed the five most qualified candidates. The only two candidates with any formal administrative experience are interviewed, but dismissed for various reasons. The interviewing team has selected two finalists but is divided on which one would be the better fit for the new school and best serve in the capacity as the assistant. Maureen has strong feelings toward one of the two candidates. While she sees one as a mirror image of herself, she admits the other has complementary traits that would make a well-rounded teammate.

One finalist is Jamie Patte, a fifth-grade teacher at a neighboring progressive suburban elementary school. She is in her ninth year of teaching, all in Grade 5 in the same district. Most recently,

Jamie completed her administrative certification program through a prestigious state university. Jamie's references describe her as organized, dependable, creative, accepting, trusting, and nurturing. These traits surfaced during her first-round interview through her interactions with committee members and responses to the various questions. During a tour of the new building, Jamie was curious about its layout, noted some possible safety issues, and asked insightful questions about how the building meets the needs of the students and programs.

The second finalist is Dwayne Boren, a seventh-grade language arts teacher at a middle school in an urban district. He has 10 years of teaching experience spanning Grades 6–8 mainly in language arts, but also has taught study skills and coached middle school basketball. He completed his administrative certification program at a large urban university with a positive reputation. Dwayne's references describe him as assertive, positive, decisive, confident, and determined. During the interview, the committee was impressed with his intelligence and the level of confidence that came from Dwayne's responses. The committee members also remarked on his self-confidence and how engaging he was throughout the entire process.

Questions

1. Based on leadership traits, which of the two candidates do you believe is most like Maureen? Use specific traits to justify your response.

2. Explain why the candidate not chosen in Question 1 may be more complementary and less a mirror image. Use specific traits to justify your response.

3. The committee is composed of educators and parents. What traits from each candidate do you think most appeal to the teachers? What traits from each candidate do you think most appeal to the parents?

(Continued)

(Continued)

Advanced Questions

4. Maureen was identified as an effective building leader, thus being transferred to the head principal position in the new building. Do the traits she has justify her success? Explain.

5. In what ways could the weaknesses of the trait approach affect the selection of a candidate and his or her long-term success in this role?

6. Draft a letter to Maureen explaining which candidate should be hired with a basis on leadership traits to support your decision.

—Thomas Starmack, Bloomsburg University

CASE 2.2

WHY CAN'T DARIN LEAD?

Darin Dawkins is frustrated. He has been an assistant vice president in advancement for Springfield Community College for the past 14 years, serving under two vice presidents. Both times that the vice president's job was open, Darin applied for it and, while considered and interviewed by the selection panel, wasn't chosen for the job.

It was announced this week that his current boss, Betsy Williams, will be leaving to become the president of Flynn University, a small private college in the Northwest. The community college staff and faculty all say that Betsy will make a great college president: She is highly intelligent, very extraverted, and confident. The only female on SCC's President's Cabinet, she exhibited a strong determination to successfully make her mark in what many considered to be an "old boys' club." Under her leadership, SCC had its first successful capital campaign, raising $12 million for a new science building. The faculty at the college highly approve of Betsy, saying she seems more authentic than any of the other cabinet members. Staff like her as well; she is sought out as a mentor by a number of young professionals from other departments.

Darin, on the other hand, has felt he has been languishing in Betsy's shadow. The job of vice president is a high-profile position, encompassing the departments of alumni relations, development, and college marketing and communications. Betsy is always on the go, meeting with donors, legislators, the media, and high-powered individuals who can help move the college forward. Darin keeps a lower profile, often staying in his office, happily working on spreadsheets or researching and writing grant applications. He is a very successful grant writer, having brought in more than $4 million in the past three years. People who work on projects with him describe him as extremely competent and highly ethical. He is liked

(Continued)

(Continued)

by faculty, but none of them seek him out for advice or guidance with work issues. In general, the advancement staff see Darin as "a nice guy" but not really a go-getter. Outside the department, Darin's name is familiar to faculty and staff, but no one is really sure what he does at the college.

Darin has decided to approach Betsy for her input on how he can become the next vice president. She is well aware that it is a job Darin really wants and, more so, believes after 14 years he deserves. In their meeting, Betsy starts out by asking Darin what leadership qualities he has that he believes will make him successful as the vice president.

Darin thinks a minute and says, "I have a lot of experience in this area. I've worked here for 14 years."

"That's true, and that's valuable," Betsy responds with a nod. "But what personal characteristics do you have that you think will make you a good leader?"

"Well, I am a hard worker," Darin answers. "I stay late and work on weekends to get the job done. And I am good at grant writing and understand more about the finances of the College Foundation than anyone."

Betsy nods again. "Yes, you are a hard worker and very good with the numbers. If I asked the other members of our office what your strengths are, what do you think they would tell me?"

Darin gets very quiet. After a moment of reflection, he says, "Well, I think they like me, don't you?"

"Yes," Betsy answers. And waits. When Darin doesn't offer anything more, she says, "Darin, I know you applied for the vice president's job the last time it was open, and I was hired. Why do you think I was chosen over you?"

Darin becomes a little flustered, his face turning red. "Really, I don't know," he stammers. "I thought maybe it was because you were a woman, and they wanted to have some diversity."

Betsy is quiet for a moment, then says gently, "Well, Darin, I don't believe that's why they hired me. And I am sure I haven't been hired to be Flynn University's president just because I am a woman."

Embarrassed, Darin stands up. "I appreciate your time, Betsy," he says as he turns and quickly leaves her office.

Questions

1. What leadership traits does Betsy exhibit that make her successful in her position as vice president?

2. Which of the major leadership traits does Darin have?

3. How would you suggest Darin improve on the major leadership traits he may lack?

Advanced Questions

4. Compare and contrast Betsy's and Darin's emotional intelligence.

5. Compare and contrast Betsy and Darin using the *Big Five personality factors*. Does the differences in their personalities explain why Betsy is in a leadership position and Darin is not? Explain your answer.

6. While traits are important for leadership, what *behaviors or styles* of leadership does Darin have that could make him an effective vice president?

—Authors

REFERENCE

Northouse, P. G. (2019). *Leadership theory and practice* (8th ed.). Thousand Oaks, CA: SAGE.

3

Skills Approach

If you are engaged in learning to be an educator, such as working on a college degree in the field or taking professional development courses to improve your competencies and knowledge, then you subconsciously believe in the premises of the skills approach.

Like the trait approach discussed in Chapter 2, the skills approach takes a leader-centered perspective on leadership. However, the skills approach shifts from a focus on personality characteristics, which usually are viewed as innate and largely fixed, to an emphasis on skills and abilities that can be learned and developed. Although personality certainly plays an integral role in leadership, the skills approach suggests that knowledge and abilities are also needed for effective leadership.

Skills are what leaders *can accomplish*, whereas *traits* are who leaders *are* (i.e., their innate characteristics). Leadership skills are defined here as the ability to use one's knowledge and competencies to accomplish a set of goals or objectives. These leadership skills can be acquired, and leaders can be trained to develop them.

There are two distinct approaches when it comes to leadership skills: the early work of Katz (1955), who developed the *three-skill approach*, and the more recent work of Mumford and his colleagues (Mumford, Zaccaro, Harding, Jacobs, & Fleishman, 2000), who initiated the development of a comprehensive *skills model of leadership.*

Three-Skill Approach

Katz (1955) suggested that effective administration (i.e., leadership) depends on three basic personal skills: technical, human, and conceptual (Figure 3.1).

*Technical skill*s are knowledge about and proficiency in a specific type of work or activity. They include competencies in a specialized area, analytical ability, and the ability to use appropriate tools and techniques.

Figure 3.1   Management Skills Necessary at Various Levels of an Organization

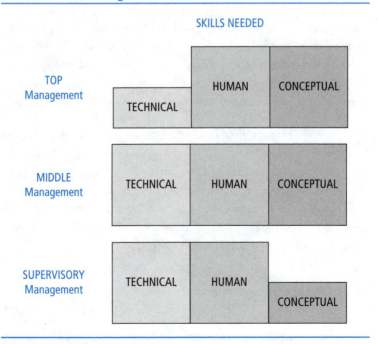

SOURCE: Adapted from "Skills of an Effective Administrator," by R. L. Katz, 1955, *Harvard Business Review, 33*(1), 33–42.

Figure 3.2 Skills Model of Leadership

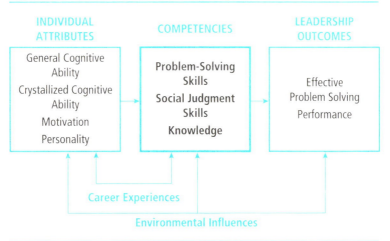

SOURCE: Adapted from "Leadership Skills for a Changing World: Solving Complex Social Problems," by M. D. Mumford, S. J. Zaccaro, F. D. Harding, T. O. Jacobs, and E. A. Fleishman, 2000, *Leadership Quarterly, 11*(1), 23.

Human skills are knowledge about and ability to work with *people.* These are the abilities that help a leader to work effectively with followers, peers, and superiors to accomplish the organization's goals. Leaders with human skills adapt their own ideas to those of others, are able to create an atmosphere of trust, and are sensitive to the needs and motivations of others.

Conceptual skills are the ability to work with abstract ideas and concepts. A leader with conceptual skills is comfortable talking about the ideas that shape an organization and the intricacies involved, putting goals into words, and working with abstractions and hypothetical notions. Conceptual skills are central to creating a vision and strategic plan for an organization because they provide an understanding of what a company stands for and where it is or should be going.

Skills Model of Leadership

A second approach to skills leadership developed by Mumford and his colleagues (2000) is more complex than Katz's paradigm. This model, outlined in Figure 3.2, delineates five components of effective leader performance: *competencies, individual attributes, leadership outcomes, career experiences,* and *environmental influences.* The leader competencies at the heart of the model are *problem-solving skills, social judgment skills,* and *knowledge.* These competencies are directly affected by the leader's individual attributes, which include the *leader's general cognitive ability, crystallized cognitive ability, motivation,* and *personality* as well as his or her *career experiences* and *the environment.* The model postulates that effective problem solving and performance can be explained by the leader's basic competencies and that these competencies are in turn affected by the leader's attributes, experience, and environment.

CASE STUDIES

The following case studies provide descriptions of leadership situations in educational settings that can be evaluated from the skills perspective. The first case addresses the skills required by a school district's after-school program coordinator. In the second case, a panel weighs the different skills of candidates for a coordinator to lead a new college program.

At the end of each case, you will find two sets of questions that will help in analyzing the case. The first set can be answered using information provided in this chapter; the second set, Advanced Questions, provides an opportunity for deeper exploration of the skills approach to leadership and is designed to coincide with the concepts discussed in Chapter 3 of *Leadership: Theory and Practice* (8th ed., pp. 43–72).

CASE 3.1

BEFORE BARB BURNS OUT

Barb Margolin is the coordinator of after-school programs for 11 elementary schools in Johnson County Public Schools. A former fourth-grade teacher, Barb was thrilled to take the coordinator position. She supervises a team of youth development specialists to plan and implement academic interventions, enrichment programs, student clubs, and other activities for the students to engage in during the three hours immediately following the end of the school day. Barb is responsible for a variety of tasks, including hiring staff, budgeting, curriculum development, developing community partnerships, and grant monitoring. Barb works with individuals at every level of the district, including students, support staff, teachers, and principals, reporting to the assistant vice president of academic services.

Barb had a great first year in the program. The people she worked with liked her, saying she was fun to be around, said yes to every project request, and knew all the students and their family members by name. Barb developed strong working relationships with her colleagues and a positive connection with the school staff. She came up with some creative new activities for the students, and students in the academic intervention programs started showing improvement. Sometimes Barb fell behind on getting paperwork completed and let a deadline for a task slip, but her supervisor and others gave her the benefit of the doubt, recognizing it was her first year in the job and she was learning the position.

Barb's second year as coordinator is not going as well. Paperwork has piled up, and tasks she needs to do are falling through the cracks. Recently, an important deadline for a grant contract was missed, costing the program about $40,000. This is the third time in as many months Barb has missed a deadline. In addition, several principals have told Barb's supervisor that Barb seems overwhelmed and unable to follow through on promises she made to them. Barb continues to innovate the program, but several of the changes she instituted this year required more attention from her during their implementation. Hand-holding these changes has taken her energy and attention away from other responsibilities.

Barb's demeanor has suffered as well. Those who work with her say that she once was very upbeat and positive, but now seems stressed and overwhelmed. She still says yes to every project request, but fewer and fewer projects are actually being completed.

Her supervisor knows Barb brings valuable skills to this position, but must help her develop other needed skills before Barb burns out completely.

Questions

1. Based on Katz's three-skill approach to leadership (Figure 3.1), how would you describe Barb's technical, human, and conceptual skills? In which of these is she the strongest?

2. Given the duties and tasks in her position, would you character-ize Barb's job as supervisory, middle, or top management? Which skills does she need to work on in order to perform at that level?

3. Looking at the three components of the skills model of leadership (Figure 3.2), describe Barb's strongest individual attributes and competencies. How do these relate to the outcomes of her leader-ship (i.e., effective problem solving and performance)?

4. How does her environment and career experience affect Barb's leadership?

5. As Barb's supervisor, how would you work on developing the skill areas she may be lacking?

—Trevor J. Davies

PICKING A PROGRAM LEADER

Northern State University's Department of Student Services' new Firsts Program is designed to help low-income and first-generation students, as well as those who come from the foster care system, learn to navigate college. The public university created the program after it found that many of its students who come from these backgrounds dropped out of college after their first year.

The department conducted a study with former students from these backgrounds to identify the obstacles that made college difficult for them and discovered that, for many of them, college is an unfamiliar landscape. Things such as how to apply for financial aid (when they don't have parents with tax returns), balancing school and jobs, and knowing how to access school resources such as email accounts and computers, were completely new to them. One young woman said, "I knew nothing about how to 'go to college.' I just showed up at my first class with a pen and notebook and was stunned to find out that everyone had already bought the book and read the first chapter. I didn't even know where or what the bookstore was."

Another student, a former foster child, lived in the dorms and was stunned to find out the dorms were closed for three weeks over the holidays: "I didn't have anywhere to go, so I used every last dime I had to stay at a really crappy hotel. I felt abandoned and embarrassed."

The Firsts Program will be overseen by a coordinator who will work one-on-one with each student in the program to help him or her succeed. The panel choosing the coordinator has three candidates for the position:

Lucy Wallis has worked in the Department of Student Services for 10 years as an assistant program director. Before that she was a student at the university and worked as a resident adviser in the dorms and as an orientation leader. She is very knowledgeable of the university and the services it provides. She is also very familiar with faculty, which is a plus when it comes to working with them to help students. Lucy has a good understanding of the university's bureaucracy—she knows which faculty and staff members to talk to in order to achieve things, but also has a grasp of the unwritten rules of working with the administration. Lucy's references say she is very likable, with great people skills, and she has always had positive performance evaluations.

Wynter Simmons does not come from within the college. She is a caseworker with the city's Department of Social Services and works exclusively in cases dealing with child placement. She is a former foster child who has a master's degree and is working on a doctorate. A graduate of Northern State, she is knowledgeable of many of the services available, but doesn't have a basic understanding of how to work with college programs and administration. In her interview, Wynter presented a clear direction for the new program, outlining her goals and how she would go about achieving them. Some of her references have said that Wynter can be abrupt and a little abrasive with colleagues, but is nothing but compassionate when working with the children in her caseload. Three of the foster students she has managed are now attending the university, and she is credited with helping them succeed.

Geno Polydoris also works within the university. He is currently an assistant coach and the student athlete mentor for the Department of Athletics. His job is to work with student athletes to keep up their academics and playing eligibility. Geno is the first in his family to graduate from college; he went to Northern State on scholarship as a running back on the football team. In his interview, Geno explained that many of the student athletes he works with come from situations similar to those in the Firsts Program. Many are first-generation college students, many come from low-income families where college wasn't ever discussed as a future option, and two were actually homeless before they came to Northern State. Geno has focused on helping the athletes receive extra academic help, teaching them basic life skills like money and time management and working with them to balance schoolwork and athletics. While generally respected, Geno has had a few testy interactions with faculty and staff on

(Continued)

(Continued)

campus who think he asks for special allowances for those he mentors because they are athletes. But the numbers don't lie: Northern State's student athletes have higher GPAs and graduation rates than the national average for college athletes.

The head of the selection panel summed up the search this way: "It's a good problem to have. We have three highly skilled candidates, and the choice won't be easy."

Questions

1. Using Katz's three-skill approach as illustrated in Figure 3.1, compare Lucy, Wynter, and Geno in terms of their technical, human, and conceptual skills. In which skill area is each candidate strongest and weakest?

2. Is one of these skills—technical, human, or conceptual—most important for the Firsts Program coordinator to have? Explain your answer.

Advanced Questions

3. Looking at the three components of the skills model of leadership as illustrated in Figure 3.2, compare Lucy, Wynter, and Geno in terms of their *individual attributes* and *competencies* for this job.

4. How would you compare Lucy, Wynter, and Geno in regard to the environment and their career experiences? How do these factors influence their leadership potential?

5. Skills can be learned. What skills do Lucy, Wynter, and Geno each need to learn in order to be successful in the coordinator position?

– Authors

REFERENCES

Katz, R. L. (1955). Skills of an effective administrator. *Harvard Business Review*, *33*(1), 33–42.

Mumford, M. D., Zaccaro, S. J., Harding, F. D., Jacobs, T. O., & Fleishman, E. A. (2000). Leadership skills for a changing world: Solving complex social problems. *Leadership Quarterly*, *11*(1), 11–35.

4

Behavioral Approach

INTRODUCTION

Was your favorite teacher a taskmaster who provided directions and structure, or someone who was more laid back and nurturing? Chances are it was the educator who was both, able to balance the times when students needed to be kept on task with the times students needed nurturing and emotional support—often doing these simultaneously.

These behaviors—task behaviors and relationship behaviors—are at the heart of the behavioral approach to leadership. The behavioral approach to leadership focuses exclusively on *what leaders do* and *how they act toward followers* in various contexts. Researchers studying the behavioral approach determined that leadership is composed of two general kinds of behaviors: *task behaviors* and *relationship behaviors*. Task behaviors facilitate goal accomplishment while relationship behaviors help followers feel comfortable with themselves, with each other, and with the situation in which they find themselves. How leaders combine these two types of behaviors to influence others is the central focus of the behavioral approach.

The behavioral approach originated from three different lines of research: the Ohio State studies, the University of Michigan studies, and the work of Blake and Mouton on the Managerial Grid®. Researchers at Ohio State developed a leadership questionnaire called the Leader Behavior Description Questionnaire (LBDQ), which identified *initiation of structure* and *consideration* as the core leadership behaviors. The Michigan studies provided similar findings but called the leader behaviors *production orientation* and *employee orientation.*

Using the Ohio State and Michigan studies as a basis, much research has been undertaken to find the best way for leaders to combine task and relationship behaviors. The goal has been to find a universal set of leadership behaviors capable of explaining leadership effectiveness in every situation. Unfortunately, it's not that easy, and researchers have had difficulty identifying one best style of leadership.

A third line of research on leadership behaviors was begun by Blake and Mouton in the early 1960s exploring how managers used task and relationship behaviors in the organizational setting. Blake and Mouton developed a practical model for training managers that described leadership behaviors along a grid with two axes: *concern for results* and *concern for people* (Figure 4.1). This model has been used extensively in organizational training and development.

How leaders combine these orientations results in five major leadership styles: authority–compliance (9,1), country-club management (1,9), impoverished management (1,1), middle-of-the-road management (5,5), and team management (9,9). Blake and Mouton (1985) indicated that people usually have a dominant grid style that they use in most situations and a backup style. The backup style is what the leader reverts to when under pressure, when the usual way of accomplishing things does not work.

The behavioral approach reminds leaders that their actions toward others occur on both a task level and a relationship level. In some situations, leaders need to be more task oriented; in others, they need to be more relationship oriented. Similarly, some followers need leaders who provide a lot of direction, whereas others need leaders who can show them a great deal of nurturance and support. Overall, the behavioral approach reminds leaders that their impact on others occurs through the tasks they perform as well as in the relationships they create.

Figure 4.1 The Leadership Grid

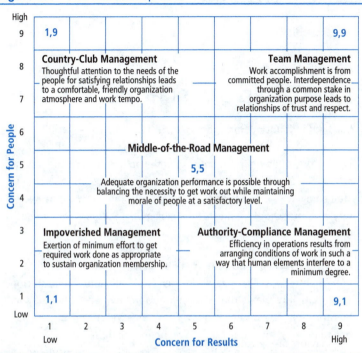

SOURCE: The Leadership Grid© figure, Paternalism figure, and Opportunism figure from *Leadership Dilemmas—Grid Solutions*, by Robert R. Blake and Anne Adams McCanse (formerly the Managerial Grid by Robert R. Blake and Jane S. Mouton). Houston, TX: Gulf (Grid figure: p. 29, Paternalism figure: p. 30, Opportunism figure: p. 31). Copyright 1991 by Scientific Methods, Inc. Reproduced by permission of the owners.

CASE STUDIES

The following case studies describe leadership situations in educational settings that can be evaluated from the behavioral perspective. The first case describes the head of a private school who eschews technology. In the second case, two college professors have different methods for mentoring a student struggling with his student teaching.

At the end of each case, you will find two sets of questions that will help in analyzing the case. The first set can be answered using information provided in this chapter; the second set, Advanced Questions, provides an opportunity for deeper exploration of the behavioral approach to leadership and is designed to coincide with the concepts discussed in Chapter 4 of *Leadership: Theory and Practice* (8th ed., pp. 73–94).

CASE 4.1

SPRINGFIELD DAY SCHOOL

Ella Lindon founded Springfield Day School when she was 33. Now, nearly 40 years later, the school is everything she dreamed. Nestled in a historic building in a quiet residential neighborhood, the private school has 100 students in preschool to eighth grade. The Springfield staff consists of Ella, her administrative assistant, a part-time secretary, two preschool teachers, nine classroom teachers (one in each grade), and teachers for music, PE, and art.

The school has very low attrition. Ella picks the students (and their families) herself. There is a lengthy application process, during which Ella interviews the children and families, and it is Ella who has the final say on admission. Families stay at Springfield Day because they feel that they have been specially selected from among many to join an elite group. They speak with pride when they say, "Ella chose us to come here," "Ella's wonderful," and "We would do anything for Ella."

Springfield Day's curriculum and programming reflect Ella's particular biases, most notably her attitude toward technology. She has no use for it in her own life, and has begrudgingly found a place for it in the pre-K–8 curriculum. There are computers in each classroom connected to the Internet. While the older students use technology to create multimedia projects, the computers in the younger students' classrooms sit mostly unused. But what is most shocking to new families is that the use of email at the school is strictly forbidden. Ella has often said that messages are communicated better and more accurately when people speak directly to each other. She also is an advocate of the "lost art of letter writing," saying that the personal touch is more effective. As a result, parents who wish to communicate with staff or teachers must call or come to the school to talk to them, and communication from the school to families comes in the form of weekly printed newsletters or phone calls. The parents are even discouraged from exchanging email addresses with one another, though they confess in whispers that they do, because it makes arranging play dates easier.

Ella communicates with her staff entirely through handwritten notes. All day long, student runners take turns delivering communiqués from Ella, written on her signature heavy-bond, pale blue stationery. The notes may include words of praise, a comment about a student, or questions. Sometimes they are task oriented: reminders that progress reports are due, requests for meetings, or questions about projects in process. In general, though, Ella doesn't need to write very many task-oriented notes. Ella often brags about her faculty's autonomy and her hands-off approach, saying that the staff have been there so long they know what is expected and when.

Most of the faculty have been with the school for 20 years or more; the newest hire joined the school 10 years ago. All were handpicked by Ella and are accustomed to her "management by note" method. The teachers all say they feel supported and often go to Ella with concerns, both school-related and personal. She knows them, their histories, and their families. She listens and offers advice, and helps them find the resources they need to address their concerns. Ella frequently treats the staff to lunch after conferences or other major events during the school year.

The first-grade teacher, Stacey, has announced she will retire this year. Ella has interviewed five potential replacements, all candidates in their 20s. When told about the technology restrictions at the school and Ella's management by note, three of the candidates withdrew from the search, one declaring incredulously in the interview, "How do you get anything done without computers and email?"

Ella just shrugs. Her philosophy and method has worked for 40 years, and Springfield Day is thriving with a long waiting list for admission.

(Continued)

(Continued)

Questions

1. Where would you place Ella on Blake and Mouton's Leadership Grid (Figure 4.1)?

2. Would you describe Ella as more task oriented or relationship oriented?

3. Why do you think Ella's behavioral leadership approach has been successful for Springfield Day School?

Advanced Questions

4. Would you describe Ella as having a maternal orientation in her leadership behavior? Give examples to support your answer.

5. As new faculty come on board who have less experience than the current teachers, what are some obstacles they may encounter with Springfield Day's management methods?

6. Ella is 73 and will retire at some point, but there is no succession plan in place. Do you think Ella should be replaced with an internal candidate who shares her leadership philosophies or with an outside candidate? What leadership behaviors should the ideal candidate have in order to continue the school's success?

—Anne Lape, Educator

CASE 4.2

MENTORING JACK

Frank Melville was a classroom teacher for 15 years before earning his PhD in education. He now teaches pre-service teachers and supervises intern teachers in the field. Frank enjoys the work and feels he's making a greater impact than he did as a classroom teacher. Most of the students he works with have done well in their coursework, but when they get into the classroom, they find being a teacher is not as easy as they had expected. They discover teaching is more than just knowing the subject matter and explaining it to students and expecting them to sit at rapt attention while they do it. After a semester working in the classroom with their supervising teachers, most of the interns are ready to take over their own classrooms. But some are not, and that's where Frank's real work begins.

Allison Bradford works alongside Frank with pre-service and intern teachers. Allison went straight from undergraduate work in English to earning a PhD in education. Her only teaching experience came from her work as an intern teacher. However, articles she has authored on mentoring pre-service teachers are widely published in respected journals.

Frank and Allison disagree on how to assist the struggling teachers. Frank advocates that the most essential attribute of a great teacher is his or her ability to be what he calls "a presence in the classroom." This quality is what allows excellent teachers to command students' attention with a glance or a few words and hold their attention without shouting or using tricks like clapping. Frank believes that most great teachers are born with this ability, but those who don't have it can develop it with practice, consideration, and time. Frank seeks to help students do so by reflecting with them on their teaching practice so that when they have classrooms of their own, the day-to-day choices they make as teachers will be instinctual.

(Continued)

(Continued)

Allison, on the other hand, firmly believes that good teachers are made—by understanding foundations, being organized, and completing set tasks, almost anyone can become an excellent teacher. Allison's classes focus on educational theory and history, and her students write in-depth research papers and detailed curriculum plans. Allison feels that sending interns into the classroom armed with facts, theories, and solid curricular knowledge will better prepare them to make informed decisions as teachers.

This semester, Frank and Allison have been asked to work together to mentor Jack Clayton, an intern English teacher in his second internship, having failed his first. Jack is bright, but tends to ramble on as he lectures and is unable to keep his students engaged. He is often unprepared for class, he has difficulty giving students feedback on their work, and his own work can be sloppy. His classroom management is nonexistent; he does not know how to control the students or to get them to comply with his expectations.

Frank and Allison have very different methods for mentoring Jack. Frank meets daily with Jack to talk about what happened that day in Jack's classroom, to discuss what went well and why, and to explore strategies for Jack to handle difficult situations he encountered. Frank observes Jack's classes regularly and makes an effort to praise Jack's improvements and efforts, no matter how small, and to provide Jack with constructive feedback.

Allison's method involves having Jack script each day's lesson plans a week ahead of time and schedule activities down to the nearest five minutes. She has Jack develop an elaborate discipline plan and implement it in his classroom, instructing him to leave no gray areas. Allison also observes Jack's class once a week and provides him with further written assignments and readings to improve what she views as his weak areas.

Jack's teaching improves. He comes to school more prepared, his lessons are more organized, and the students are better behaved, because the consequences for ill behavior are harsh. But Jack's teaching still lacks passion, he doesn't enjoy teaching, and the students aren't enjoying learning. Jack looks forward to his talks with Frank, because he is by nature a reflective person. He likes the idea of what he could accomplish in the classroom, but still isn't certain how to get from his discussions with Frank to a teaching career that he'll enjoy.

Questions

1. Is Frank a task- or relationship-oriented leader? What about Allison?

2. Using Blake and Mouton's Leadership Grid (Figure 4.1), where do you think Frank would score? And Allison?

3. What leadership style from the grid do you think would be best to use with Jack?

Advanced Questions

4. Based on Jack's classroom management and abilities when he first started, where would you place him on Blake and Mouton's Leadership Grid? What about after he received mentoring? Defend your answer.

5. Frank and Allison are approaching mentoring Jack using different leadership behaviors. How could they work together to help Jack?

6. Do you think it is possible for Jack to be an effective teacher if he doesn't feel the passion for the field or like teaching? Explain your answer.

—*Anne Lape, Educator*

REFERENCES

Blake, R. R., & McCanse, A. A. (1991). *Leadership dilemmas: Grid solutions.* Houston, TX: Gulf.

Blake, R. R., & Mouton, J. S. (1964). *The Managerial Grid.* Houston, TX: Gulf.

Blake, R. R., & Mouton, J. S. (1978). *The new Managerial Grid.* Houston, TX: Gulf.

Blake, R. R., & Mouton, J. S. (1985). *The Managerial Grid III.* Houston, TX: Gulf.

5

Situational Approach

When third-grade teacher Arianna G. moved into middle school to teach seventh grade, she found a new set of leadership challenges. The rewards she had successfully used to motivate her third graders—extra recesses, a class party when they achieved their reading goals, a "prize bucket" of various trinkets that students could choose from when they learned their math facts—would never work with middle schoolers. For one thing, there are no recesses at her middle school. And trinkets? Can you just imagine the adolescent eye rolls?

This is the premise behind the situational leadership approach: Different situations demand different kinds of leadership. One of the more widely recognized approaches to leadership, situational leadership posits that to be effective, a leader must adapt his or her style to the demands of different situations and individuals under his or her leadership (Blanchard, 1985; Blanchard, Zigarmi, & Zigarmi, 1985; Hersey & Blanchard, 1969, 1993).

Situational leadership is a prescriptive approach, stressing that leadership is composed of both a *directive* and a *supportive* dimension and that each has to be applied appropriately in a given situation. To determine what is needed in a particular situation, a leader must evaluate her or his followers and assess how competent and committed they are to perform a given task. Based on the assumption that followers' skills and motivation vary over time, situational leadership suggests that leaders should change the degree to which they are directive or supportive to meet the changing needs of followers.

This situational approach to leadership classifies leadership into different styles based on directiveness and supportiveness. The styles include leaders who act highly directive with low support, highly directive with high support, low directive with high support, and low directive with low support. The situational approach also describes how each of the four leadership styles applies to followers who, for a particular goal, may be at different levels of competence and commitment, including low in competence and high in commitment, moderately competent and low in commitment, moderately competent but lacking commitment, and having a great deal of competence and a high degree of commitment.

The situational approach to leadership provides specific prescriptions for what leaders should do in various situations. For example, if an elementary school has a new teacher who is just out of college and very excited about teaching but is unfamiliar with the school's rules and procedures, the leader (principal) should be directive with the new teacher, orienting him or her to the school and all the details regarding the school day, teaching plans, discipline, and dealing with parents. On the other hand, this same principal might have several experienced teachers who are highly committed and very competent in their roles when it comes to certain goals. The situational approach suggests that in these cases the principal should allow the teachers to be on their own and do what they think needs to be done without directions from the principal.

Using our earlier example of Arianna G., she could argue that when it comes to understanding class assignments, her third graders are less competent and committed while her seventh graders are probably more competent and committed, needing less direction and support. Effective leadership occurs when the leader can accurately diagnose followers' needs and abilities in a task situation and then exhibit the prescribed leadership style that matches that situation. As educators, we will have students and staff who are at different levels working simultaneously together, and it is the effective educational leader who can motivate and lead across the different levels.

CASE STUDIES

The following case studies help illustrate how situational leadership can be applied in educational settings. In the first case, a school principal has two teachers who use different approaches to bring up state assessment scores. The second case addresses how the director of a university enrollment management office must get disparate departments to work together.

For each of these cases, ask yourself what you would do if you found yourself in a similar situation. At the end of each case, you will find two sets of questions that will help in analyzing the case. The first set can be answered using information provided in this chapter; the second set, Advanced Questions, provides an opportunity for deeper exploration of the situational approach to leadership and is designed to coincide with the concepts discussed in Chapter 5 of *Leadership: Theory and Practice* (8th ed., pp. 95–116).

CASE 5.1

A TALE OF TWO TEAMS

Living in the age of educational accountability, Jorge Hernández, principal of a regional public high school, is feeling the pressure from his district's superintendent to improve student performance on state assessments. Due to the large student and staff population at his high school, Jorge knows he cannot successfully mine all the student achievement data and develop approaches to address deficient areas by himself. Last year, he took a hands-off approach and charged the English and math department heads with data analysis and distribution of data to the teachers, an assignment that each department head approached differently.

The English department chair, Tamika Jones, assembled her department members two times a month, providing the teachers with the initial data and asking them to organize the data in a manner that made sense to them. Tamika then charged the teachers to collect additional formative assessment data to monitor student progress. Based on the data, teachers modified curriculum and instructional practices to target standards not being achieved by students. Because of what they were seeing, the teachers requested a language arts lab be established to help students who scored below proficient, and Tamika found the resources to create the lab. She also allowed the teachers to control the data, make changes, and own the solutions to improve the current status of student performance. She provided various supports when necessary, such as minor schedule or room changes and release time, and made a point to celebrate staff and student success.

Lewis Milton, the math department chair, took a different approach. Lewis reviewed the initial data, wrote reports that identified areas of concern, and then distributed his reports to the math teachers in an initial meeting. He instructed the teachers to use the data reports to change their instruction to improve student performance in the indicated areas of concern. Lewis told the teachers that he would make

(Continued)

(Continued)

classroom visits and be available during planning time to assist with strategies and resources. Midway through the year, he held one additional meeting with the teachers to discuss the data. Minutes from teachers' meetings held during the year revealed that some of the math department teachers were frustrated and had not received the attention they requested from Lewis, while others reported they were experiencing good progress and liked having autonomy to address student performance on their own.

As Jorge reviews the most recent state assessment scores, he notes there has been a significant growth in language arts, while math scores have remained stagnant. As a new school year approaches, Jorge realizes that he must make changes in the approaches taken to bring up the assessment scores. He plans to have individual meetings with each department chair and then meet with them together to develop an action plan for the new school year.

Questions

1. How would you describe the leadership styles of Tamika Jones and Lewis Milton? How do they differ in terms of directiveness and supportiveness?

2. How would you describe Jorge's leadership style in this situation?

3. If you were Jorge, how would you approach the separate meetings you plan to have with Tamika and Lewis? How would you approach the meeting with both of them together?

Advanced Questions

4. For this assignment, at what development levels are Lewis and Tamika? At what level are their followers?

5. Use specifics from the descriptions of the various situational leadership styles in the text to explain why Tamika's approach was successful.

6. What leadership style should Jorge use in his upcoming meetings with Lewis and Tamika?

—Thomas Starmack, Bloomsburg University

CASE 5.2

INTEGRATION HESITATION

Jackie Weller is the recently hired director of enrollment management at Southeast Community College. In her position, Jackie is charged with identifying enrollment goals for the college that are aligned with SCC's multiple missions, strategic plan, environment, and resources. Enrollment management, which seeks to maximize enrollment at the college while ensuring the college's future viability, involves the college's administrative processes, student services, curriculum planning, and market analysis. This is the first time SCC has had an enrollment management position, and Jackie knows that enrollment management is not just about recruitment; it is about retaining students and measuring student outcomes during all phases of the enrollment process. It's an effort that requires constant review, evaluation, and problem solving, and Jackie is expected to influence others at the college in participating in advancing enrollment initiatives.

Jackie has reviewed the college's enrollment management processes and come to the conclusion that the admissions and financial aid offices, which have separate staffs, directors, and technology, need to be integrated. With the rising cost of college and growing student debt, admissions officers are finding that addressing the issue of cost of college for prospective and current students is paramount. They can't do that without an understanding of financial aid options and processes. At the same time, the financial aid team is constantly challenged by an ever-changing system and the need to balance spending between merit- and need-based financial aid.

Jackie sees integrating the two offices as an important step in improving service because it would make a "one-stop shop" concept for students who are enrolling. Students would only have to visit one office to wade through the information and paperwork they need in order to enroll at the college.

(Continued)

(Continued)

Integrating the two offices has many layers: Not only will both teams need to be cross-trained on the operations of the other office; there will also be communication issues, co-sharing of office space, and the bringing together of two separate technology systems. In addition, many of the team members are designated "specialists" at the college, and Jackie knows that this new approach will be stretching the "specialist" role by asking team members to adopt more of a generalist role.

Corey Doran, the director of admissions, is 100% on board, supportive of Jackie's integration plan, but he can't say that for all of his team members. His counterpart, Jenna Jackson, the director of financial aid, is very resistant to Jackie's plan, and most of her staff are as well. Jenna is very concerned about maintaining the confidentiality levels of financial aid data that her office adheres to and says she doesn't feel she could guarantee those same levels if the admissions staff were trained in the financial aid systems. Jenna has also made it clear to Jackie that she isn't sure how financial aid fits into the bigger picture of enrollment management and why they would need to integrate with admissions staff.

Jackie starts by providing articles on enrollment management to Corey and Jenna, including several that specifically outline the reasons and roles where financial aid and admissions offices work together. She also sent Jenna and Corey to the same national conference on enrollment management practices where they attended several days of workshops and programs. Both Jenna and Corey then separately attended conferences outside their disciplines: Corey attended a financial aid conference while Jenna spent a week at an admissions conference.

When they returned, Jackie had Jenna and Corey conduct a joint brainstorming session with the admissions and financial aid staff to generate ideas for integrating the two offices. Jackie stayed out of the way, believing team members would have greater ownership of ideas they generated rather than those she would put forth. At one point, however, Jackie did speak up: She brought up the concerns about confidentiality, putting the issue front and center, asking team members to detail the pros and cons about the integration from this perspective.

At the end of the brainstorming session, team members who were interested in cross-training signed up for a pilot project, where they would provide input on methods that worked for cross-training and improvements that could be made. At the same time, Jackie prioritized the list of ideas generated in the session. She began implementing the "quick wins," such as having Jenna and Corey coauthor an email message about scholarships to prospective students and having the teams collaborate on developing financial aid publications for the parents of prospective students, before taking on the more complicated integration items.

This process has taken several months, and despite all these efforts, Jenna and a few members of her team are still vocally resistant to the changes. Jackie hopes, as the process continues to evolve over time, they will become more comfortable with the new way their business is being done.

Questions

1. From a situational leadership perspective, describe where Jackie, Jenna, and Corey stand regarding integrating the two offices. What about the staff in the financial aid and admissions offices?

2. How would you describe Jackie's leadership style in this situation?

3. How effectively or ineffectively did Jackie perform her diagnosis of the situation? How did this affect how she proceeded?

Advanced Questions

4. At what developmental levels were Jenna and Corey when Jackie first started the integration process? What about their respective staff members? Where would you put their development levels by the end of the case?

5. What elements of flexibility were included in the situational example? To what extent was flexibility incorporated?

6. Jackie chose to concentrate her efforts on not only the office leaders (Jenna and Corey) but their staffs as well. Explain why you think she selected that approach over a direct, one-to-one coaching approach with just Jenna and Corey.

—Christopher W. Tremblay

REFERENCES

Blanchard, K. H. (1985). *SLII®: A situational approach to managing people.* Escondido, CA: Blanchard Training and Development.

Blanchard, K., Zigarmi, P., & Zigarmi, D. (1985). *Leadership and the One Minute Manager: Increasing effectiveness through situational leadership.* New York, NY: William Morrow.

Hersey, P., & Blanchard, K. H. (1969). *Management of organizational behavior: Utilizing human resources.* Englewood Cliffs, NJ: Prentice Hall.

Hersey, P., & Blanchard, K. H. (1993). *Management of organizational behavior: Utilizing human resources* (6th ed.). Englewood Cliffs, NJ: Prentice Hall.

6

Path–Goal Theory

INTRODUCTION

Education is very much a goal-oriented profession. From a teacher developing lesson plans to school administrators implementing new student assessment programs, setting and achieving goals permeates all levels of education. Our job as educational leaders is to provide the motivation to our staff and students to achieve those goals.

Motivation is the underlying premise of the path–goal theory of leadership. Path–goal theory puts much of the onus on leaders in terms of designing and facilitating a healthy environment to propel followers toward success. It focuses on the most effective ways a leader can motivate followers and guide them down a path to accomplish designated goals. The overriding theme of path–goal theory is that leaders need to provide "what is missing" for followers. When the road is made smoother, followers will more easily reach their goals.

Drawing heavily from research on what motivates followers, path–goal theory illuminates the relationship between a leader's behavior

51

Figure 6.1 The Basic Idea Behind Path–Goal Theory

Obstacle(s)

Followers   Path   Path   Goal(s) (Productivity)

Path–Goal Leadership

- Defines goals
- Clarifies path
- Removes obstacles
- Provides support

SOURCE: Reprinted from "Path-Goal Theory" in Northouse, P. G., *Leadership: Theory and Practice*, 8th ed. (2019), p. 118, Thousand Oaks, CA: SAGE. Reprinted with permission.

and the characteristics of the followers and the organizational setting. According to House and Mitchell (1974), leadership generates motivation when it increases the number and kinds of payoffs that followers receive from their work. For the leader, the imperative is to use leadership behaviors that best meet followers' motivational needs. Leaders try to enhance followers' goal attainment by providing followers with information or rewards they think followers need to reach their goals. Leadership also motivates when it makes the path to the goal clear and easy to travel through coaching and direction, removing obstacles and roadblocks to attaining the goal, and making the work itself more personally satisfying (Figure 6.1).

Also understanding which leader behaviors can help followers along the path to their goals is key to path–goal theory. By selecting specific behaviors and leadership styles that are best suited to followers' needs and to the situation in which followers are working, leaders can increase followers' expectations for success and satisfaction.

To that end, path–goal theory provides a set of general recommendations based on the characteristics of followers and tasks for how leaders should act in various situations if they want to be effective. Table 6.1 illustrates how leadership behaviors are related to follower and task characteristics

Table 6.1 Path–Goal Theory: How It Works

Leadership Behavior	Follower Characteristics	Task Characteristics
Directive Provides guidance and psychological structure	Dogmatic Authoritarian	Ambiguous Unclear rules Complex
Supportive Provides nurturance	Unsatisfied Need for affiliation Need for human touch	Repetitive Unchallenging Mundane
Participative Provides involvement	Autonomous Need for control Need for clarity	Ambiguous Unclear Unstructured
Achievement Oriented Provides challenges	High expectations Need to excel	Ambiguous Challenging Complex

SOURCE: Reprinted from "Path–Goal Theory" in Northouse, P. G., *Leadership: Theory and Practice*, 8th ed. (2019), p. 123, Thousand Oaks, CA: SAGE. Reprinted with permission.

in path–goal theory. Path–goal theory suggests that each type of leader behavior has a different kind of impact on followers' motivation. Whether a particular leader behavior is motivating to followers is contingent on the followers' characteristics and the characteristics of the task.

The principles of path–goal theory can be used by educators at all levels and for all types of tasks. To apply path–goal theory, educators must carefully assess their followers and their tasks, and then choose an appropriate leadership style to match those characteristics. Path–goal theory can be useful because it continually reminds educators that their central purpose is to help staff and students define their goals and then reach those goals in the most efficient manner.

CASE STUDIES

The following case studies provide descriptions of leadership situations in educational settings that can be analyzed by applying the concepts and information from path–goal leadership. In the first case, a superintendent has to bring along three diverse stakeholders in her attempts to implement a new model for education in her district. The second case looks at the efforts of a university department chair to change his program and the conflicts that result.

At the end of each case, you will find two sets of questions that will help in analyzing the case. The first set can be answered using information provided in this chapter; the second set, Advanced Questions, provides an opportunity for deeper exploration of the path–goal theory of leadership and is designed to coincide with the concepts discussed in Chapter 6 of *Leadership: Theory and Practice* (8th ed., pp. 117–138).

CASE 6.1

IMPLEMENTING A NEW MODEL FOR EDUCATION

Nancy Jefferson is the superintendent of a medium-sized public school district. Nancy is passionate about finding ways to better prepare her district's students for life after high school graduation. While the district's current teaching methods are in accordance with the state-mandated curriculum and her district's students are testing comparable to those in other school districts within the state, many of the district's graduates cannot find jobs or take the next step to begin their professional careers. After many conversations with local employers, Nancy has determined that the district's schools do not have the curriculum or facilities to produce students with the types of skills needed by the region's employers.

Economic prosperity within the region has made new financial resources available for the school district. There have been many conversations among school administrators and the school board regarding whether to use this extra funding to renovate school buildings or to build a new school. Nancy sees this as an opportune time for the district to use some of these resources to develop a new education model that will better prepare its students to meet the needs of local employers. For Nancy, the question is not "Which buildings need renovation?" but rather "How can we fund the development of a new, first-rate model of education and the facilities needed to house it?"

A local university was gifted a parcel of land that would be an ideal location for a new school within the district. Nancy and the university's president have agreed that the university would give the land to the school district to build a new, unique school. In return, the university would use the new building during the evenings and weekends for classes. This is a win-win for both the university and

(Continued)

(Continued)

the school district: The university needs more space but does not have the funding for a new building; the school district will save money by not having to buy land to build a new school.

Before any of these building plans can be put into effect, however, Nancy must gain approval from three key constituent groups to develop the new model of education:

- *The school board.* The board's support is necessary to formalize the agreement with the university and give approval to use the district's increased financial resources for this purpose. The board members are elected and are all very sensitive to how they are perceived by the voting public. Nancy would describe this group as "very control-oriented"—they like to present ideas for any innovation and change in the district as their own rather than crediting the superintendent or other administrators. The school board will soon enter the "discovery phase" of considering the proposal, which includes community meetings to listen to all constituent groups. Nancy wants to make sure the board is firmly committed to the model before this occurs.

- *Teachers.* The support of the district's teachers is essential because they will be tapped to teach the modified curriculum at the new school. A group of senior teachers who are well respected within the district and influential with the less experienced teachers have expressed skepticism about the new curriculum, saying they do not fully understand the vision or how radically modifying the current curriculum will help students. Nancy suspects some of these teachers are afraid of the additional burdens learning a new curriculum and tasks will put upon them while others may fear radical changes to their teaching methods. Many of these teachers just like to come to work and do what they have always done.

- *District students and their parents.* A sizable group of parents do not see the new school as a good fit for their children and are opposed to using the resources for a new school building. Many of these parents believe that the best future for their children is college, but the district has a 30% high school dropout rate. In addition, of the district's graduates who go on to college, only 40% of them finish with a degree. The parents won't like to hear it, but these statistics bear out that college isn't the best option for a portion of the district's students. Nancy also knows that when students who drop out of college return home, they are not prepared to work for local employers.

Nancy believes parents can be swayed if their children are motivated; however, only a small percentage of district students are supportive of the new school while many are simply indifferent. It is Nancy's belief that part of their indifference may be lack of knowledge about the kind of jobs that could await them after high school. She thinks that forging internship and job-shadowing programs for students with local employers could create some excitement as well as new appreciation for companies.

If any of these key constituent groups does not support the concept, Nancy's vision for an innovative new school will flounder. She knows one group can easily influence the other, so she must approach each constituency in a systematic way, appealing to what will motivate the group.

Questions

1. Leadership is about influencing people to reach a common goal. What are the common goals for Nancy, the school board, teachers, and students in this case?

2. What follower characteristics do you think each of the constituent groups exhibits?

3. What leader behaviors (directive, supportive, participative, or achievement-oriented) should Nancy use with each of the constituent groups she is trying to influence?

Advanced Questions

4. Path–goal theory suggests that *participative leadership* is best when tasks are ambiguous and followers are autonomous and

(Continued)

(Continued)

have a strong need for control. How could Nancy exhibit participative leadership? What impact would it have on the different groups of followers?

5. *Achievement-oriented leaders* establish high standards of excellence for followers and seek continuous improvement. How effective would achievement-oriented leadership be with the different groups Nancy is leading? Explain.

6. In looking at the path Nancy must take to reach her goal, how would you go about motivating these groups? Feeling competent and valuing outcomes is an important part of what makes people feel motivated. How could Nancy help her followers feel competent and value their work?

—John Baker, Western Kentucky University

CASE 6.2

CONFLICT WITH THE DEAN

Peter Helms is chair of the Technology Department, one of the largest and most popular departments at State University. On the outside, the department looks good: It has two of the public university's largest undergraduate programs, highly selective graduate programs, and a long history and reputation for outstanding research, which has generated millions of dollars in external grant funding.

However, Peter sees the department a little more realistically. Over the years, the external grant funding the department has received— and become dependent on for financing its robust research agenda— has eroded away. Faculty no longer focus on winning big research grants, choosing instead to pursue their personal, and less financially lucrative, research interests. The department has developed a reputation on campus for being difficult to work with, due to the perceived arrogance of its faculty and staff. On top of all this, Peter has ongoing issues with the dean of the college that governs his department.

Peter's conflict with Dean Manion has evolved over a number of years and focuses mostly on the dean's stated desires for the Technology Department to develop more outreach programs and an online degree as well as return to its aggressive pursuit of external grant funding.

It is Peter's belief, however, that the Technology Department needs to go in a different direction, especially if it wants to remain relevant. The name of the department is outdated and doesn't represent how the department's curriculum and pedagogy have evolved in the past 10 years. Both Peter and his senior faculty are resistant to changing the current pedagogy of teaching in the classroom. And while he agrees with the dean on the need for faculty to move off their personal research agendas to pursue more external grant funding, Peter knows that the faculty need new technology to

(Continued)

(Continued)

attract those grants—technology for which the college hasn't got the money to buy.

Peter has determined the only way to achieve the needed changes for his department is to move the Technology Department to another college within the university. Without Dean Manion's or his own faculty's knowledge, Peter initiated discussions with the dean of another college at the university about the possibility of moving the department there. The talks advanced to the point where Peter wrote a white paper outlining the advantages of moving the department. Once written, Peter distributed the white paper to his faculty with explicit guidance that it not be shared outside the department.

The faculty had mixed opinions regarding Peter's proposal. The senior faculty, over whom Peter has considerable influence (as he has promoted most of them during his tenure), are unanimously in favor of the name change and moving to another college. This group also has considerable influence with key university administrators. Other tenured faculty had mixed reactions; some favor the proposed change as it may result in more research opportunities for them, while others are loyal to the college that houses their tenure. The junior, untenured faculty were afraid to voice an opinion for fear of upsetting their departmental mentors or Dean Manion, both of whom have input on their future promotions and tenure.

The conflict between Peter and Dean Manion reached a critical point when the dean anonymously received and read a copy of the white paper. Saying he had lost confidence in Peter's ability to lead the Technology Department, Dean Manion immediately removed Peter as department head and appointed another faculty member as interim chair over the objections of outraged senior faculty.

Removing Peter did not quell the issue, however; the ball had already started rolling. After several months of negotiations and with the approval of the university administration, the Technology Department split. Approximately half of the faculty remained in the Technology Department under Dean Manion's college while the rest went with the new department, named the Department of Information Innovation, to another college.

Questions

1. Using the concepts of path–goal leadership, explain whether or not you feel Peter is an effective leader.

2. Path–goal leadership is about defining goals, clarifying a path, removing obstacles, and providing support for followers. What steps did Peter take (or not) in these areas regarding his goals for the department? In which of these areas could he have improved his leadership?

3. Which of these steps did Dean Manion take (or not) regarding his goals for the department? In which of these areas could he have improved his leadership?

Advanced Questions

4. When the formal authority system in an organization is weak or unclear, leaders can help followers by making the rules and work requirements clear. How would you describe the authority system at State University? How did this system affect Dean Manion and Peter?

5. Clearly, Dean Manion's leadership was ineffective with Peter. Based on Peter's attitudes and actions, what style of leadership (i.e., directive, supportive, participative, achievement-oriented) could the dean have used with Peter? Explain.

6. If you were Peter's leadership coach, how would you have helped him with this conflict? What mistakes did he make as a leader? What are his strengths?

7. Based on the principles described in path–goal theory, what leader behaviors could Peter have used with the various faculty groups (senior-committed, tenured-mixed, junior, nontenured) to increase his influence and establish more commitment to his proposal?

—John Baker, Western Kentucky University

REFERENCES

House, R. J., & Mitchell, R. R. (1974). Path–goal theory of leadership. *Journal of Contemporary Business, 3*, 81–97.

Northouse, P. G. (2019). *Leadership theory and practice* (8th ed.). Thousand Oaks, CA: SAGE.

7

Leader–Member Exchange Theory

INTRODUCTION

At its core, leader–member exchange (LMX) theory is an approach that looks at leadership from a relationship perspective. LMX theory puts the focus on the *interactions* between leaders and followers, examining the special, unique relationships that leaders create with followers and how these relationships affect organizational performance and group dynamics.

We've seen LMX theory at work in all levels of the education discipline. From a teacher who oversees a math class of 25 students of varying abilities and motivation to a college president who works with many stakeholders from alumni and donors to students, faculty, and the community in advancing the college's goals, LMX theory shows how leaders can have different relationships with different followers and how the quality of these different relationships can affect an organization. When these relationships are of high quality, the goals of the leader, the followers, and the organization are all advanced.

Figure 7.1 Dimensions of Leadership

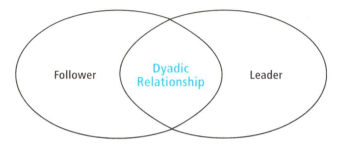

SOURCE: Reprinted from *Leadership Quarterly, 6*(2), by G. B. Graen & M. Uhl-Bien, "Relationship-Based Approach to Leadership: Development of Leader-Member Exchange (LMX) Theory of Leadership Over 25 Years: Applying a Multi-Level, Multi-Domain Perspective" (pp. 219–247). Copyright © 1995, with permission from Elsevier.

NOTE: LMX theory was first described 28 years ago in the works of Dansereau, Graen, and Haga (1975), Graen (1976), and Graen and Cashman (1975). Since it first appeared, it has undergone several revisions, and it continues to be of interest to researchers who study the leadership process.

LMX theory works in two ways: It describes leadership, and it prescribes leadership. In both instances, the central concept is the *dyadic relationship* (Figure 7.1) that a leader forms with each of his or her followers.

In-Groups and Out-Groups

In the early studies of LMX theory, a leader's relationship to followers was viewed as a series of vertical dyads, categorized as being of two different types: Leader–member dyads based on expanded role relationships were called the leader's *in-group*, and those based on formal job descriptions were called the leader's *out-group*. According to LMX theory, followers become in-group members based on how well they get along with the leader and whether they are willing to expand their role responsibilities. Followers who maintain only formal hierarchical relationships with their leader become out-group members. Whereas in-group members receive extra influence, opportunities, and rewards, out-group members receive standard job benefits.

Table 7.1 Phases in Leadership Making

	Phase 1 Stranger	Phase 2 Acquaintance	Phase 3 Partnership
Roles	Scripted	Tested	Negotiated
Influences	One way	Mixed	Reciprocal
Exchanges	Low quality	Medium quality	High quality
Interests	Self	Self and other	Group

Time →

SOURCE: Adapted from "Relationship-Based Approach to Leadership: Development of Leader–Member Exchange (LMX) Theory of Leadership Over 25 Years: Applying a Multi-Level, Multi-Domain Perspective," by G. B. Graen & M. Uhl-Bien, 1995, *Leadership Quarterly, 6*(2), p. 231.

Leadership Making

Another emphasis in LMX research has been on leadership making, which stresses that leaders should try to develop high-quality exchanges with all of their followers. The leadership-making model developed by Graen and Uhl-Bien (1991) shows that leadership making develops over time and includes a *stranger phase*, an *acquaintance phase*, and a *mature partnership phase* (Table 7.1). By taking on and fulfilling new role responsibilities, followers move through these three phases to develop mature partnerships with their leaders. These partnerships, which are marked by a high degree of mutual trust, respect, and obligation, have positive payoffs for the individuals themselves, and help the organization run more effectively.

Leadership making is a prescriptive approach to leadership emphasizing that a leader should develop high-quality exchanges with all of his or her followers rather than just a few. It attempts to make every follower feel as if he or she is a part of the in-group and, by so doing, avoids the inequities and negative implications of being in an out-group.

Leadership making suggests leaders go beyond their own areas and create high-quality partnerships with people throughout the organization as well. LMX theory can be used to explain how individuals create leadership networks throughout an organization to help them accomplish work more effectively (Graen & Scandura, 1987). A person with a network of high-quality partnerships can call on many people to help solve problems and advance the goals of the organization.

When applied to education, the basic premise of LMX theory is that teachers need to be aware of how they relate to all of their students. It tells teachers to be sensitive to whether some students receive special attention and some students do not. In addition, it tells teachers to be fair to all students and allow each of them to become as involved in the work of the class as they want to be. LMX theory promotes building respectful and trusting relationships with every student, recognizing that each student is unique and wants to relate to his or her leader in a special way.

CASE STUDIES

The following case studies help to clarify how LMX theory can be applied to leadership situations in educational settings. The first case is about a fourth-grade teacher, while the second is about an adviser for a student organization at a university, and both cases examine how leaders may treat groups differently within an organization.

At the end of each case, you will find two sets of questions that will help in analyzing the case. The first set can be answered using information provided in this chapter; the second set, Advanced Questions, provides an opportunity for deeper exploration of the LMX theory of leadership and is designed to coincide with the concepts discussed in Chapter 7 of *Leadership: Theory and Practice* (8th ed., pp. 139–162).

CASE 7.1

FAVORITISM IN THE CLASSROOM

Aidan Dennis is the head of a charter school in a suburban town. The school is very successful, and part of its success is its small class size (no more than 16 students per class), experienced teachers, and very involved parent group.

A month after school started, one of the mothers, Donna Andrews, approached Aidan about a problem she perceived was going on in Mr. Mitchell's fourth-grade classroom. Donna's daughter Emma had been coming home every day from school in tears about the unfair treatment that she feels Mr. Mitchell is meting out in his class. Of Mr. Mitchell's 15 students, 10 are girls. The girls have socially divided into two groups, each one with a distinct leader. Emma is a floater; she likes both groups of girls, and they both accept her.

Emma believes that Mr. Mitchell favors the group of girls led by Maeve, a bright and bossy 10-year-old. Maeve has a knack for relating well with adults, almost charming them. Emma claims that Mr. Mitchell favors Maeve's group, assigning them to sit together at the same table, calling on them in class more often than the other students, and letting them get away with small infractions that he doesn't let pass with the other kids.

The other group of girls is led by Abby, who struggles with ADD. The group also includes Jonetta, who is a child model and has appeared in several television commercials. Maeve and her friends facetiously call Jonetta "Ms. Movie Star" and generally avoid having any contact with her. A third girl in the group is Brie, who was good friends with Maeve in third grade. Something happened over the summer, and now Maeve doesn't talk to Brie at all.

Ms. Andrews explains that Emma has described to her mother numerous situations where Emma thinks Mr. Mitchell is being

(Continued)

(Continued)

"mean" to Abby, saying he talks more sharply to Abby than he does to the other kids. Emma is a very empathetic girl, and the mistreatment of any of her friends greatly upsets her. Emma believes that because Abby is their friend, Jonetta and Brie are also treated differently by Mr. Mitchell.

Aidan decides to spend the next morning in Mr. Mitchell's classroom. After everyone has settled in, Maeve pops up to Mr. Mitchell's desk and offers to hand out the morning work to everyone, which he gladly lets her do. As the students are doing their work, they are talking to their tablemates. Aidan observes that Maeve and her friends are just as loud as the other students, yet Mr. Mitchell calls out the students at other tables, telling them to "quiet down" or "do less talking, more working."

Later, Mr. Mitchell conducts a writing exercise, where students are given a list of vocabulary words, look up the words' meaning in the dictionary, and then write sentences using the words. When the sentences are completed, Mr. Mitchell asks, "Who wants to share the sentence they wrote using this word?" and calls on students who raise their hands. Aidan observes that all four of the girls at Maeve's table are called upon to answer, but only one from Abby's group. Mr. Mitchell then calls on the boys in the class to provide the rest of the sentences. Aidan also observes that after all the girls at Maeve's table have been called on, the girls in Abby's group stop raising their hands to provide answers.

Mid-morning the class heads outside for a short recess. At one point, Abby and two of her friends jog up to Mr. Mitchell. "Remember in science how we talked about those bugs that can disguise themselves?" Jonetta asks excitedly. "We found one of those moths on that tree! Come look." At the same time, however, two boys in a group throwing a football around start tussling.

Without replying to the girls, Mr. Mitchell starts walking quickly toward the boys, shouting, "Max and Jackson, get your hands off each other!" Abby and the other girls are obviously dismayed when Mr. Mitchell walks away from them. Emma, who is sitting nearby reading a book, says consolingly, "It's OK, Jonetta. He just needs to go keep them from fighting."

After recess, the students work on math problems. Mr. Mitchell walks around the room, watching students work. He laughs at something funny the girls at Maeve's table say and praises a couple of the boys. When he comes to Abby's table, he stands there for a while watching them work. Aidan observes that Abby seems to tense up. Where she had been quietly working on her problems, now she seems distracted and unable to focus. The other girls at the table keep their heads down working on their sheets, saying nothing to one another.

"Don't forget to show your work," Mr. Mitchell says, moving away to the next group.

Questions

1. Based on the principles of LMX theory, what observations would you make about Mr. Mitchell's leadership in the classroom?

2. Is Donna Andrews justified in raising concerns regarding how Mr. Mitchell is treating her daughter Emma? Explain.

3. Identify the in-group and the out-group in this situation.

Advanced Questions

4. At what phase of leadership making would you place Mr. Mitchell and his relationship with Abby's group and his relationship with Maeve's group?

5. In what way is Mr. Mitchell's relationship with the different groups productive or counterproductive to his being a classroom leader?

6. If you were Aidan, how would you advise Mr. Mitchell about his approaches with the different groups in the classroom? What would you suggest Mr. Mitchell do differently?

—Authors

CASE 7.2

WHO GETS TO BE THE STUDENT CONSULTANTS?

Students for Nonprofit Consulting (SNC) is a successful student organization based in the College of Business at Northwest State College. Open to all students on campus regardless of their academic major, SNC provides free business consulting services to nonprofit organizations based within a 50-mile radius of Northwest State. Students are attracted to volunteer with SNC because it not only gives them real-world experience, but also provides training courses in topics such as volunteer management, nonprofit finances, and marketing, which are taught by the group's adviser, Dr. Ashley Williams. Ashley, a business faculty member, has volunteered her time with SNC for more than 10 years, and has developed close working relationships with several students through her advising work.

SNC has grown steadily both in requests for service from the local community and in the number of students interested in volunteering. However, Ashley has been asked to meet with the provost for her perspective on an anonymous complaint lodged by a campus donor and parent of a Northwest student. The complaint claims that SNC has a highly stilted assignment system for matching students to nonprofits, which results in a lack of opportunity for growth for some volunteers. Moreover, the complainant is threatening to make his complaint public if action isn't taken soon.

In her meeting with the provost, Ashley brushes aside any concerns about lack of advancement opportunities, pointing out that several students who started in SNC without any experience have graduated with high-paying consulting jobs in large companies. She also details SNC's comprehensive matching system, where students request available consulting opportunities and are placed with organizations based on their preferences and availability after the student leadership team (a group of experienced SNC students who work even more closely with Ashley) come to consensus on assignments.

While the provost is relieved to hear of these initiatives, Ashley still feels uneasy. In response, she invites several SNC students enrolled in one of her business courses to a conference room to discuss the allegations. Many of the students express surprise and disagreement with the allegation, countering that they believe Ashley works hard to make SNC a welcoming organization. They share several instances of how Ashley's informal mentoring helped them to build their consulting skills and become stronger leaders. The students say they feel particularly strongly that Ashley's trust in and respect for them has helped them grow, and are surprised that others might not feel the same.

Although their responses ease Ashley's discomfort somewhat, she decides to bring up the issue at the next SNC general meeting, where she asks all SNC members to provide their thoughts on SNC's advancement opportunities and consulting assignment system. While many members share comments similar to those Ashley has already heard, a minority of nonbusiness students seem withdrawn during the discussion. After the meeting, she approaches one of these students, Carlos, a junior in psychology who is active on campus. Carlos struggles to make eye contact with Ashley while he admits that he agrees to some extent with the complaining parent. He describes a handful of instances in which he did not learn of consulting training sessions until after they had occurred. He says this negatively affected his confidence in applying for some of the more complex consulting opportunities. In addition, he mentions that while he respects the work of the student senior leadership team, he perceives that the group often gives the assignments of highest importance to those they know well and those who have been the most successful in past assignments, which makes it difficult for the less experienced volunteers to develop new skills.

Ashley is glad to hear Carlos's point of view because it provides her with a small sense of comfort. While there seems to be a need

(Continued)

(Continued)

to better promote upcoming training sessions, Ashley wants the most motivated and dedicated volunteers to be given the best opportunities. After reflecting on the situation, she decides to provide the students responsible for promoting the training courses a more rigorous schedule to adhere to, but otherwise opts to keep SNC's processes the same.

Questions

1. Based on the LMX perspective, how would you describe Ashley's leadership as the SNC adviser?

2. Are the allegations raised by the anonymous parent/donor justified? Explain.

3. Are there in-groups and out-groups in SNC? Describe the in-groups and out-groups and Ashley's relationship to them.

Advanced Questions

4. In what ways is Ashley engaging in "leadership making" in her work as the group's adviser? In what ways could she improve her leadership making?

5. Do you agree with Ashley's solution of providing the students responsible for promoting the training sessions with a more rigorous schedule to adhere to, but otherwise keeping SNC's volunteer matching process the same? Is it a good one for building relationships with her followers? Discuss.

6. Do you agree with Ashley's approach of asking students for their input on the allegations? By doing so, did Ashley breach any confidentiality issues?

—David Rosch, University of Illinois
at Urbana-Champaign

REFERENCES

Dansereau, F., Graen, G. B., & Haga, W. (1975). A vertical dyad linkage approach to leadership in formal organizations. *Organizational Behavior and Human Performance, 13*, 46–78.

Gerstner, C. R., & Day, D. V. (1997). Meta-analytic review of leader-member exchange theory: Correlates and construct issues. *Journal of Applied Psychology, 82*, 827–844.

Graen, G. B. (1976). Role-making processes within complex organizations. In M. D. Dunnette (Ed.), *Handbook of industrial and organizational psychology* (pp. 1202–1245). Chicago, IL: Rand McNally.

Graen, G. B., & Cashman, J. (1975). A role-making model of leadership in formal organizations: A developmental approach. In J. G. Hunt & L. L. Larson (Eds.), *Leadership frontiers* (pp. 143–166). Kent, OH: Kent State University Press.

Graen, G. B., & Scandura, T. A. (1987). Toward a psychology of dyadic organizing. In B. Staw & L. L. Cumming (Eds.), *Research in organizational behavior* (Vol. 9, pp. 175–208). Greenwich, CT: JAI.

Graen, G. B., & Uhl-Bien, M. (1991). The transformation of professionals into self-managing and partially self-designing contributions: Toward a theory of leadership making. *Journal of Management Systems, 3*(3), 33–48.

Graen, G. B., & Uhl-Bien, M. (1995). Relationship-based approach to leadership: Development of leader–member exchange (LMX) theory of leadership over 25 years: Applying a multi-level, multi-domain perspective. *Leadership Quarterly, 6*(2), 219–247.

8

Transformational
Leadership

INTRODUCTION

At its very core, education is about transformation. It is a process that changes and transforms people. Education is one of the few fields where transformational leadership is practiced on every level from nearly the minute an educator steps foot on a campus or in a classroom.

Transformational leadership provides a general way of thinking about leadership that emphasizes ideals, inspiration, innovations, and individual concerns. The emphasis in the transformational leadership approach is on intrinsic motivation and follower development, focusing on emotions, values, ethics, standards, and long-term goals. A transformational leader is attentive to the needs and motives of followers and tries to help followers reach their fullest potential.

Most all of us have experienced a special educator or teacher (such as a counselor, orchestra director, or coach) who was transformational. These individuals were special because they challenged us to do our best. They accepted us for who we were, trusted us, and saw us as valuable. They were someone we could always talk to who never judged us and seemed to model who we wanted to be. Because of these truly special educators, we felt like somebody. Even years later, these are the educators we want to go back and visit.

When we talk about transformational leaders, we are describing leaders like those special people above. Transformational leaders are change agents who are good role models, can create and articulate a clear vision, empower followers to meet higher standards, act in ways that make others want to trust them, and give meaning to organizational life. At the same time, transformational leaders are aware of how their own behavior relates to the needs of their followers and the changing dynamics within their organizations. Recent research by Mason, Griffin, and Parker (2014) has found that transformational leadership can result in positive psychological gains for both leader and follower.

Bass (1985) developed four factors that are present in transformational leadership: idealized influence or charisma, inspirational motivation, intellectual stimulation, and individualized consideration (Table 8.1).

As you can see in Table 8.1, transformational leadership provides a broad set of generalizations of behaviors and actions that are typical of leaders who are transforming or who work in transforming contexts. Expanding on these, researchers have identified a number of behaviors and actions that fall into these categories including empowering followers and nurturing followers in change, having a highly developed set of moral values, exhibiting confidence and competence, being articulate and able to express strong ideals, creating and communicating a shared vision for the organization, and encouraging others and celebrating their accomplishments.

An encompassing approach, transformational leadership can be used to describe a wide range of leadership from very specific attempts to influence followers on a one-to-one level to very broad attempts to influence whole organizations and even entire cultures. And just as it is for an educator in a classroom, the transformational leader plays a pivotal role

Table 8.1   Four Factors of Transformational Leadership

Factor 1: Idealized Influence	Also known as *charisma*, describes leaders who act as strong role models for followers.
Factor 2: Inspirational Motivation	Describes leaders who communicate high expectations to followers and provide inspirational motivation, including building a sense of team spirit.
Factor 3: Intellectual Stimulation	Describes leaders who stimulate followers to be creative and innovative and to challenge their own beliefs and values as well as those of the leader and the organization.
Factor 4: Individualized Consideration	Describes leaders who provide a supportive climate by listening carefully to the individual needs of followers and act as coaches and advisers.

SOURCE: Adapted from *Leadership and Performance Beyond Expectations*, by Bernard M. Bass, 1985, New York, NY: Free Press.

in precipitating change, but followers and leaders are inextricably bound together in the transformation process.

CASE STUDIES

The following case studies describe leadership situations in educational settings in which transformational leadership is present. The first case describes the leadership involved in transitioning an elementary school into a magnet school. The second case looks at the role charisma plays in the leadership of a university president.

At the end of each case, you will find two sets of questions that will help in analyzing the case. The first set can be answered using information provided in this chapter; the second set, Advanced Questions, provides an opportunity for deeper exploration of transformational leadership and is designed to coincide with the concepts discussed in Chapter 8 of *Leadership: Theory and Practice* (8th ed., pp. 163–196).

CASE 8.1

CREATING A MAGNET SCHOOL

Joan is the principal of the 600-student Broadhurst Elementary School, a public school in a midsize city. Joan's school district is undergoing federally mandated desegregation efforts. The district has applied for, and received, funding to create four unique magnet schools. Each school will have its own theme and programming in hopes of attracting new students, stabilizing the student population, and raising the district's profile.

Joan's school has been designated as a magnet school for writing. The teachers will teach different genres and forms of writing using the Writer's Workshop approach. This will differ from the way writing is taught at other elementary schools in the district. Under the district's agreement with its teachers' union, any current teacher at Broadhurst who wishes to may transfer to another building, but no teacher will be required to leave. All of the teachers at Joan's school have chosen to stay as it transitions to being a magnet school.

In the process of applying for the federal money, a proposal was developed for Broadhurst Magnet School that included a tentative curriculum, plans to remodel the library to include a computer lab and performance space, a budget for materials, and adding a curriculum coordinator to the staff.

Over the summer, Kate, the new curriculum coordinator, and a core group of four of the school's teachers work together to refine the new curriculum and plan and implement back-to-school professional development for the rest of the teachers to bring them on board with the new program.

Once the school year starts, tensions start to rise. It becomes clear that many of the teachers stayed at Broadhurst not because they are committed to the school's new mission, but because the idea of transferring to another school was unappealing. A number of

(Continued)

(Continued)

teachers are resistant to teaching writing in the curriculum's new more open-ended manner and object to what they consider to be lax standards regarding publishing children's work that is still in developmental stages and not teacher-corrected to perfection. Other teachers object to the increase in their workloads because they have had to learn the new curriculum without any other duties being taken off their teaching plates.

Joan was a classroom teacher and a reading specialist before becoming a principal, and empathizes with her staff. She is a "hands-on" principal, who arrives at school at 6 a.m. and does not leave until after 6 p.m. each night. She comes in on Saturdays to work and open the school for teachers who wish to work in their rooms. During school days, she is rarely found in her office; but instead, she is in classrooms, talking to and working with students. She monitors lunch periods herself. She has a strong rapport with each staff member and supports each teacher in his or her areas of strength, encouraging all of them to seek out professional development, team teach, and try new programs and techniques. The elementary school building features a variety of team teaching configurations, with each team determining the division of duties among members. Other teachers who prefer to teach independently are equally supported and encouraged.

Joan sets high standards for her staff. The new curriculum expectations are clearly laid out, and while she is willing to discuss them, she expects these standards to be met. She supports the team of teachers who developed the curriculum and defers to their opinions as questions arise.

Joan places a great deal of trust in her new curriculum coordinator, Kate. It's Kate's job to train each teacher to use the Writer's Workshop method in his or her classroom. Kate is responsible for planning programming, writing grants, and ensuring that the overall program runs smoothly. When teachers complain to Joan about the new curriculum and expectations, she listens and then reminds them of their decision to stay at Broadhurst. If they are struggling, she encourages them to accept help from Kate. She also works to help the teachers find ways to make their teaching satisfying by giving them recognition for good work that they do, no matter how small the accomplishment. Joan believes that this helps reinforce that teaching is sometimes a series of small victories rather than large ones.

On the flip side, when Kate is struggling with getting a particular teacher to follow the program, Joan listens to Kate's concerns and provides suggestions on how to work with that teacher more successfully. For example, Joan knows that one teacher is more responsive to written feedback than verbal, so Joan suggests that Kate give the teacher her ideas for improvement in writing a few days before she meets with her.

A year after they begin the process of transitioning to the magnet school model, the school receives a positive assessment from federal evaluators. Just as rewarding, Joan, Kate, and the leadership team are invited to the National Magnet School Conference to speak about their transition process.

Questions

1. How is this an example of transformational leadership?

2. Using examples, explain the aspects of transformational leadership (*idealized influence, inspirational motivation, intellectual stimulation*, and *individualized consideration*) that Joan exemplifies.

3. A transformational leader is attentive to the needs and motives of followers and tries to help followers reach their fullest potential. Give examples of how Joan and Kate employ these qualities in their leadership.

Advanced Questions

4. Discuss whether Joan and Kate's leadership is transformational or transactional.

5. Based on Joan's leadership style, do you think that the success of her program was ensured, or was there a possibility for failure?

6. How did Joan's trust in her team contribute to the success of the program?

—Anne Lape, Educator

IS CHARISMA ENOUGH
FOR PRESIDENT STELAR?

Dr. Jerri Stelar achieved her dream job when she became the president of her alma mater 20 years after graduating. A distinguished career in higher education administration, most of it in fund-raising and creating relationships with influential stakeholders, has prepared Dr. Stelar to lead the public university. Her passion for her alma mater, coupled with her professional experience, was viewed by constituents as critically needed by the university.

Initially, Dr. Stelar easily won people over with her relational leadership skills and enthusiasm for the university. Charismatic, especially when relating to others one-on-one, Dr. Stelar quickly became popular with people throughout the university from the maintenance personnel to the Board of Trustees. She articulated over and over that her focus was to develop the university into an institution that attracted the best students and elevate it from a regional university to a force that competed with prestigious universities on a national level. Dr. Stelar was extremely effective in conveying to influencers her determination to rebuild the physical campus's buildings and grounds, which had been neglected over the past 30 years. Funds began flowing into the university from many different sources, both private and governmental, to renovate the campus into one of the most beautiful in the state.

Dr. Stelar was also instrumental in establishing needed and desired academic programs at the university. Historically, internal state politics precluded the university from offering several key programs, such as engineering and nursing, but Dr. Stelar influenced state legislators to allow the university to offer these programs. Her collaborative efforts with more prestigious universities to offer innovative joint programs also filled voids in the university's curriculum. Both of these accomplishments were favorably received by the people in the region, but only met with neutral enthusiasm by the university's faculty.

Early in her presidency, Dr. Stelar experienced a situation where the trustees questioned her judgment. Since that experience, she has ensured that all information and actions are thoroughly vetted to ensure the trustees' support of her efforts. These actions, plus her success in the visual rebuilding of the campus, gave her the influence she needed to convince the trustees to grant her an extended employment contract that guaranteed her present position for the next decade. In addition to rewarding Dr. Stelar for her accomplishments, the extended contract was also a preventative measure by the trustees to ensure she would not leave the university for a more attractive offer.

After being granted the long-term contract, Dr. Stelar became visibly more confident as a leader as well as more demanding of those who worked with her. She still maintains superb relationships with the trustees and outside influencers and continues to make improvements to the campus. Her influence with the trustees ensures dissenting views about her efforts are either not heard or marginalized.

The faculty and staff, however, aren't as content. They are beginning to express confusion regarding the future of the university. Many still believe that the university should provide for the needs of the people in its region, while others think the university's mission is to compete on a national level. When asked, many can't identify the values or vision of the university. People feel multiple sets of values exist and, while the vision is captured in a great-sounding tag line, it is difficult to interpret. When asked at the annual State of the University meeting to explain her vision for the university, Dr. Stelar describes a somewhat vague image for the future.

Now in her 17th year, Dr. Stelar is extremely popular with the trustees, students, and other constituents. Faculty and staff, however, are becoming more disgruntled and disillusioned with the university

(Continued)

(Continued)

president. During several years of difficult economic conditions when university employees received minimal or no pay raises, there was wide speculation that Dr. Stelar received substantial pay increases that had been guaranteed in her extended contract. Enrollments that grew rapidly during the early years of Dr. Stelar's tenure are now stagnant, and despite the fact that this is similar to what most other universities are experiencing, her detractors claim it is because the university is spending too much money on buildings and not enough on academics.

For the first time since Dr. Stelar became president of her beloved university, there are those who question if she is the leader needed to create the university's pathway into the future.

Questions

1. Is this an example of transformational leadership? Explain.

2. Using examples, explain the aspects of transformational leadership (*idealized influence, inspirational motivation, intellectual stimulation*, and *individualized consideration*) that Dr. Stelar exemplifies.

3. A transformational leader is attentive to the needs and motives of followers and tries to help followers reach their fullest potential. Give examples of how Dr. Stelar employed these qualities in her leadership.

Advanced Questions

4. Would you describe Dr. Stelar as a transformational leader or a transactional leader? Explain your answer.

5. How could a lifetime contract for a key leader affect the transformational process within an organization?

6. Could Dr. Stelar be described as a pseudotransformational leader? Discuss.

—*John Baker, Western Kentucky University*

REFERENCES

Avolio, B. J., & Gibbons, T. C. (1988). Developing transformational leaders: A life span approach. In J. A. Conger, R. N. Kanungo, & Associates (Eds.), *Charismatic leadership: The elusive factor in organizational effectiveness* (pp. 276–308). San Francisco, CA: Jossey-Bass.

Bass, B. M. (1985). *Leadership and performance beyond expectations*. New York, NY: Free Press.

Mason, C., Griffin, M., & Parker, S. (2014). Transformational leadership development: Connecting psychological and behavioral change. *Leadership & Organization Development Journal, 35*(3), 174–194.

9

Authentic Leadership

We live and teach in an uncertain world. Shootings at schools, terrorism on a worldwide scope, political scandals, and economic upheaval leave our students and ourselves feeling apprehensive and insecure about what is going on around us. As a result, people long for leadership they can trust and for leaders who are honest and good.

Attention to authentic leadership is emerging in response to societal demands for genuine, trustworthy, and good leadership. Authentic leadership focuses on the authenticity of leaders and whether their leadership is genuine and "real." It is leadership that is transparent, morally grounded, and responsive to people's needs and values.

There is not a lot of agreement on what constitutes authentic leadership, but when trying to define it, three distinct viewpoints and emphases arise (Chan, 2005):

- The *intrapersonal perspective* focuses closely on the leader's self-knowledge, self-regulation, and self-concept. Shamir and Eilam (2005) suggest that authentic leaders exhibit genuine leadership,

84

lead from conviction, and are originals, not copies. This perspective emphasizes the life experiences of a leader and the meaning he or she attaches to those experiences as being critical to the development of the authentic leader.

- The *interpersonal perspective* outlines authentic leadership as relational, created by leaders and followers together (Eagly, 2005). It results not from the leader's efforts alone, but also from the response of followers. Authenticity emerges from the interactions between leaders and followers because leaders affect followers and followers affect leaders.

- The *developmental perspective* views authentic leadership as something that can be nurtured in a leader, rather than as a fixed trait. Authentic leadership develops in people over a lifetime and can be triggered by major life events and experiences. This perspective views authentic leadership as comprising four distinct but related components: self-awareness, internalized moral perspective, balanced processing, and relational transparency (Avolio, Walumbwa, & Weber, 2009), which leaders learn and develop over their lifetime (Avolio & Gardner, 2005; Gardner, Avolio, & Walumbwa, 2005; Walumbwa, Avolio, Gardner, Wernsing, & Peterson, 2008).

In addition, two approaches to authentic leadership have emerged: the *practical approach*, which provides prescriptions for how to be authentic and how to develop authentic leadership; and the *theoretical approach*, which describes what authentic leadership is and what accounts for it.

Practical Approach

On the practical side, George's (2003) approach focuses on five charac-teristics leaders should develop to become authentic leaders: (1) They have a strong sense of purpose, (2) they have strong values about the right thing to do, (3) they establish trusting relationships with others, (4) they demonstrate self-discipline and act on their values, and (5) they are sensitive and empathetic to the plight of others (i.e., act from their heart).

Figure 9.1 Authentic Leadership Characteristics

Figure 9.1 illustrates these five dimensions of authentic leadership—*purpose*, *values*, *relationships*, *self-discipline*, and *heart*—as well as the related characteristics of passion, behavior, connectedness, consistency, and compassion that individuals need to develop to become authentic leaders.

Theoretical Approach

The theoretical approach to authentic leadership identifies four major components of authentic leadership: self-awareness, internalized moral perspective, balanced processing, and relational transparency (Walumbwa et al., 2008). The theoretical perspective posits that leaders develop these attributes through a lifelong process that is often influenced by critical life events as well as the leaders' positive psychological characteristics and moral reasoning.

Authentic leadership is still in its formative phase, but recent research by Steffens, Mols, Haslam, and Okimoto (2016) found that when leaders champion the collective good, followers are more inspired, and the leader's authenticity is enhanced. In today's uncertain global climate, where people continue to search for good and sound leadership, it is a leadership approach that will continue to gain traction and attention.

CASE STUDIES

The following case studies describe individuals in educational settings who demonstrate authentic leadership qualities. The first case describes a middle school principal and his dealings with the leadership of the Parent Teacher Organization. The second case looks at the work of a campus minister.

At the end of each case, you will find two sets of questions that will help in analyzing the case. The first set can be answered using information provided in this chapter; the second set, Advanced Questions, provides an opportunity to analyze the case using ideas from authentic leadership and is designed to coincide with the concepts discussed in Chapter 9 of *Leadership: Theory and Practice* (8th ed., pp. 197–226).

CASE 9.1

PARENTS, PRINCIPALS, AND PLAYGROUNDS: OH MY!

Alex James is in his second year as an elementary principal in a rural public school district. Parents consistently remark on how passionate, approachable, and accommodating Mr. James is in regard to students and working with the community. He has built strong relationships with his teachers and demonstrates great compassion and support when staff members have personal issues.

Alex has worked hard to build relationships with parents and believes attending monthly Parent Teacher Organization (PTO) meetings is important for interacting with parents and providing support to their various initiatives. He was unable to attend the past two meetings because of other district-related meetings, but followed up with a phone call to Holly Keiser, the PTO president. On both occasions, Holly assured Alex that attendance at the meetings had been normal, agenda items were handled effectively, and everything ran smoothly.

Tonight's PTO meeting promises to be more of the same. The meeting is attended by 17 parents and six teachers. Holly leads the meeting, starting off with announcements of upcoming events and accolades to the teachers, students, and parents who assisted with the fall festival. Holly then asks if anyone has concerns to be brought before the PTO before moving ahead with the remaining agenda items. Alex finds this somewhat peculiar since new business is usually discussed at the end of PTO meetings.

MaryJo Ash, a parent of multiple children at the school, steps forward to raise a concern regarding safety on the playground. She says that many children have been injured—including two of her own—because there is not enough wood mulch under the playground equipment and that teachers are not properly supervising the children. Betty Wood, another parent known for her frequent complaining, chimes in, noting that these issues were brought up at past meetings with assurances that they would be addressed by Mr. James. She asks why they haven't been.

Holly explains that the PTO does not get involved with supervision of the playground, and parents with these concerns need to report them to the school's administration. She states that the PTO is currently working on raising funds for new mulch for the playground. During Holly's explanation, side conversations occur among the teachers in the audience and some parents, with several looking over at Alex. Alex does not want to take over the meeting or address the supervision concerns without having more information, especially since he knows the teachers who supervise the playground haven't reported any issues. Holly is careful not to have the meeting get out of control, reassuring the parents that she and Mr. James will meet afterward to discuss possible changes in playground supervision methods.

The meeting continues with three additional items: a budget report by Treasurer Aimee Wilson, an update on the current fund-raisers, and a short presentation by the local fire department on campfire safety. After the meeting adjourns, the teachers leave quickly while a few parents mill around outside the building chatting. Alex approaches Holly and Aimee. "I think the meeting went well," Holly says to him. "The same old complainers, but we have learned to ignore them."

Alex does not want to embarrass either woman, so he simply responds, "I really liked tonight's proactive approach to educating the community on campfire safety and including our local first responders in the process. I am impressed with the efforts of the parents in the various fund-raisers and the support the PTO gives our teachers, students, and school. I have some concerns regarding the playground and will have to reflect on a course of action."

Holly shakes her head. "Really, Mr. James, those two women only attend so they can complain about things. I wouldn't take their claims too seriously."

(Continued)

(Continued)

Alex smiles. "We'll look into any possible issues, just the same."

Aimee quickly jumps in, thanking Alex for his support and for attending the meeting, and then asks if he will assist her in reviewing the current revenues and expenditures prior to the next meeting. He agrees and everyone disperses.

Questions

1. Which of the two leaders, Alex or Holly, demonstrates more of an authentic leadership style? Why?

2. What specific actions or behaviors by Alex demonstrate the components of authentic leadership (*self-awareness*, *internalized moral perspective*, *balanced processing*, and *relational transparency*)?

3. What specific actions or behaviors by Holly demonstrate the components of authentic leadership (*self-awareness*, *internalized moral perspective*, *balanced processing*, and *relational transparency*)?

Advanced Questions

4. Which of the five essential authentic leadership qualities identified by George (*purpose*, *values*, *relationships*, *self-discipline*, and *heart*) does Alex exhibit? Which ones does Holly exhibit?

5. Are Alex's response to the situation and Holly's leadership characteristic of an authentic leader?

6. Does Holly have a moral responsibility to the PTO's leaders to investigate the claims about the playground? Does Alex? Why or why not?

—Thomas Starmack, Bloomsburg University

CASE 9.2

SISTER ANGELA, CAMPUS MINISTER

On college campuses around the world, campus ministry is the engagement of college students that enables them to grow in their faith and spirituality, regardless of denomination. Frequently, colleges and denominations employ campus ministers as leaders to facilitate this approach.

Sister Angela is the campus minister for Southwest State College, a small public college in a farming community. A Catholic nun, she became a campus minister 10 years ago and views her role as a teacher of the faith for the college's students and community.

Relationships and connectedness are important to Sister Angela. She is the epitome of making and facilitating connections. In addition to interpersonal connections, she connects individuals' gifts and talents to needs within the parish and student center. She focuses on providing personal counseling to the students, during which she develops trusting relationships with them. As a result of her genuine loyalty, Sister Angela has a following of current and former students.

Another hallmark of Sister Angela's campus ministry leadership is her discipline in executing day-to-day tasks. She sets a high standard of excellence for not only herself, but her students as well. For example, when she is working with a student team to plan a fall spiritual retreat, she ensures every aspect and need for a successful retreat is considered. When working with her student team, she holds all members accountable for the tasks and roles they have undertaken in executing the retreat. She is an effective role model.

(Continued)

(Continued)

While Sister Angela finds fulfillment in ministering to the college community, she also feels a strong need to expand her spirituality in other ways. Each summer, she will travel to another country, serving those from non-Christian faiths to help her gain a better understanding. Her travels have allowed her to interact with students from all racial, cultural, and ethnic backgrounds. Not only do these experiences foster her own spiritual growth, but they aid her in compassion and understanding for her campus ministry as well.

Sister Angela approaches her role as campus minister with a high level of energy, as well as compassion for the college students. At the same time, she exemplifies the values of her religious order, which include prayer, study, and ministry. Recently, however, several of the students Sister Angela has come to know have asked her about the Catholic Church's treatment of nuns and her views on its history of sexual abuse of children by priests. Several of the young women have expressed to Sister Angela that they are uncomfortable and considering leaving the Catholic Church because they view it as contradicting the church's stance on exclusivity and not a supportive place for empowering women.

Sister Angela has strong opinions about these issues. She was reprimanded once for taking part in a demonstration by nuns against the Church's treatment of the sisterhood and even considered leaving the faith. But after much reflection and prayer she believed she needed to make a difference in the lives of young people by continuing in her faith-filled work. Sister Angela, however, refuses to discuss her personal views on the Church or about her past struggles of her faith with the students, maintaining her loyalty to her religious order.

Questions

1. Would you describe Sister Angela as an authentic leader? Explain your answer.

2. What aspects of genuineness can be observed about this campus ministry leader?

3. Which of the components of authentic leadership—*self-awareness, internalized moral perspective, balanced processing,* and *relational transparency*—are a part of Sister Angela's approach?

Advanced Questions

4. How does Sister Angela demonstrate an authentic leadership that is "transparent, morally grounded, and responsive to people's needs" (Northouse, 2019, p. 201)?

5. Describe how Sister Angela exhibits the five essential authentic leadership qualities identified by George (*purpose, values, relationships, self-discipline,* and *heart*).

6. As an authentic leader, should Sister Angela share her opinions about the Church's treatment of nuns?

—*Christopher W. Tremblay*

REFERENCES

Avolio, B. J., & Gardner, W. L. (2005). Authentic leadership development: Getting to the root of positive forms of leadership. *Leadership Quarterly, 16*, 315–338.

Avolio, B. J., Walumbwa, F. O., & Weber, T. J. (2009). Leadership: Current theories, research, and future directions. *Annual Review of Psychology, 60*, 421–449.

Chan, A. (2005). Authentic leadership measurement and development: Challenges and suggestions. In W. L. Gardner, B. J. Avolio, & F. O. Walumbwa (Eds.), *Authentic leadership theory and practice: Origins, effects, and development* (pp. 227–251). Oxford, UK: Elsevier Science.

Eagly, A. H. (2005). Achieving relational authenticity in leadership: Does gender matter? *Leadership Quarterly, 16*, 459–474.

Gardner, W. L., Avolio, B. J., & Walumbwa, F. O. (2005). Authentic leadership development: Emergent trends and future directions. In W. L. Gardner, B. J. Avolio, & F. O. Walumbwa (Eds.), *Authentic leadership theory and practice: Origins, effects, and development* (pp. 387–406). Oxford, UK: Elsevier Science.

George, B. (2003). *Authentic leadership: Rediscovering the secrets to creating lasting value.* San Francisco, CA: Jossey-Bass.

Northouse, P. G. (2019). *Leadership: Theory and practice* (8th ed.). Thousand Oaks, CA: SAGE.

Shamir, B., & Eilam, G. (2005). "What's your story?" A life-stories approach to authentic leadership development. *Leadership Quarterly, 16*, 395–417.

Steffens, N. K., Mols, F., Haslam, S. A., & Okimoto, T. G. (2016). True to what we stand for: Championing collective interests as a path to authentic leadership. *The Leadership Quarterly, 27*(5), 726–744.

Walumbwa, F. O., Avolio, B. J., Gardner, W. L., Wernsing, T. S., & Peterson, S. J. (2008). Authentic leadership: Development and validation of a theory-based measure. *Journal of Management, 34*(1), 89–126.

10

Servant Leadership

INTRODUCTION

They are leaders "who put followers *first*, empower them, and help them develop their full personal capacities" (Northouse, 2019, p. 227). If you didn't know better, you might say that quote succinctly describes the characteristics of educators.

But it's actually the premise of servant leadership. The description of a servant leader reads very much like the job description for an educator: being committed to putting one's followers first, being honest with them and treating them fairly, making it a priority to listen to them and develop strong long-term relationships with them, and understanding their abilities, needs, and goals, which, in turn, allows these followers to achieve their full potential. In many ways, the discipline of education is filled with servant leaders at all levels.

Servant leadership encompasses both service and influence. A servant leader is a leader and a servant simultaneously. In our discussion of servant leadership, it is viewed as a behavior, a premise that is supported by the basic ideas of servant leadership highlighted by current scholars:

- Servant leaders place the good of followers over their own self-interests and emphasize follower development (Hale & Fields, 2007).

- Servant leaders demonstrate strong moral behavior toward followers (Graham, 1991; Walumbwa, Hartnell, & Oke, 2010), the organization, and other stakeholders (Ehrhart, 2004).

- Practicing servant leadership comes more naturally for some than others, but everyone can learn to be a servant leader (Spears, 2010).

Scholars have conceptualized servant leadership in multiple ways. According to Spears (2002), there are 10 major characteristics of servant leadership: *listening*, *empathy*, *healing*, *awareness*, *persuasion*, *conceptualization*, *foresight*, *stewardship*, *commitment to the growth of people*, and *building community*.

As illustrated in the model of servant leadership (Figure 10.1), servant leadership can be described as having three main components: antecedent conditions, servant leader behaviors, and leadership outcomes. *Antecedent conditions* that are likely to impact servant leaders include context and culture, leader attributes, and follower receptivity. The central focus of the model is seven *servant leader behaviors*: conceptualizing,

Figure 10.1 Model of Servant Leadership

SOURCE: Adapted from Liden, R. C., Panaccio, A., Hu, J., & Mouser, J. D. (2014). Servant leadership: Antecedents, consequences, and contextual moderators. In D. V. Day (Ed.), *The Oxford handbook of leadership and organizations*. Oxford, England: Oxford University Press; and van Dierendonck, D. (2011). Servant leadership: A review and syntheses. *Journal of Management, 37*(4), 1228–1261.

emotional healing, putting followers first, helping followers grow and succeed, behaving ethically, empowering, and creating value for the community. The *outcomes* of servant leadership are follower performance and growth, organizational performance, and societal impact.

In an ideal world, servant leadership results in community and societal change. Servant leaders make a conscious choice to *serve first*—to place the good of followers over the leaders' self-interests. They build strong relationships with others, are empathic and ethical, and lead in ways that serve the greater good of followers, the organization, the community, and society at large.

CASE STUDIES

The following case studies describe situations in educational settings in which servant leadership is present. In the first case, a principal hopes to instill a servant leadership aspect in mentoring new teachers. The second case examines a university's efforts to adopt a servant leadership model for its campus.

At the end of each case, you will find two sets of questions that will help in analyzing the case. The first set can be answered using information provided in this chapter; the second set, Advanced Questions, provides an opportunity to analyze the case using ideas from the servant leadership perspective and is designed to coincide with the concepts discussed in Chapter 10 of *Leadership: Theory and Practice* (8th ed., pp. 227–256).

CASE 10.1

STEWARDSHIP ABOUNDS

Lee Brown grew up in a midsize town about 50 miles from any large metropolitan area. A resilient child, Lee was only 9 when her mother died. Raised by her father and two older brothers, she helped out as much as possible with housework and other chores. Throughout her teenage years, Lee volunteered at various places around town, always performing tasks with a smile and not asking for anything in return. Lee was the first in her family to graduate from college and was hired as the social studies teacher at her hometown's public middle school.

Lee was excited to move back to her hometown and took great pride in infusing local history and events into her lessons. After 20 years as a teacher, she was asked to become her school's principal, a job she happily agreed to. As a principal, Lee prides herself on creating a welcoming atmosphere at the school and spends countless hours before and after school assisting with programs, fund-raising efforts, and tutoring students.

Five years into her principalship, Lee hired the school's first new teachers in over 25 years: Laci Ramone and Tyler Anthony. Both first-year teachers are put on the same eighth-grade team, replacing two teachers who had been at the school for more than 35 years. Laci will be teaching mathematics, while Tyler will instruct science. Lee established bimonthly meetings with the new teachers to discuss curriculum, instruction, assessment, and other issues of relevance. During the first two months, Lee's other obligations allowed her to only be present at one meeting, so she had a veteran teacher, Jeff Simpson, meet with Laci and Tyler. Those meetings were short, there was no real agenda, and neither Laci nor Tyler had any concerns. After the most recent meeting, Laci and Tyler asked Lee to cancel future meetings because they believed they could better use that time for grading papers and planning lessons.

Lee was surprised by their request and explained that she wanted to ensure their success as first-year teachers. She stated that she would let them know if the meetings would continue or not. The next day, Lee approached Jeff to ask about the meetings and what was discussed. Jeff reported that both Laci and Tyler seemed very solid and had no real concerns. He explained that during the meetings, the process of requesting supplies and textbooks was outlined, and some resources for lesson plan development were provided. Lee thanked him and stated she would handle future meetings. Later that evening, Lee returned home from a town charity organizational meeting and began creating an action plan on what supports the new teachers need and how to provide those to Laci and Tyler. She also started brainstorming on ways to empower other veteran teachers at the school to be part of the process.

Questions

1. Which of the 10 characteristics of servant leadership defined by Spears (2002) does Lee Brown exhibit? Provide examples.

2. What antecedents occurred in Lee's life that could have influenced her toward a servant leadership style?

3. Utilizing the model of servant leadership (Figure 10.1), what leadership behaviors and outcomes are present in Lee's reaction and actions to Laci and Tyler's request of canceling future meetings?

Advanced Questions

4. Following a servant leadership style, develop and defend the goals that Lee should put in her action plan to resolve the situation.

5. In the research literature, servant leadership has been conceptualized both as a trait and as a behavior. Which of these two (trait or behavior) best describes Lee's leadership in this case? Discuss.

6. There is research that shows that in some situations servant leadership is not a preferred kind of leadership. Do you think Laci and Tyler want Lee to be a servant leader? Explain your answer.

—Thomas Starmack, Bloomsburg University

A MODEL CAMPUS

When Dr. Ron Camron became president of a small, private, religious-affiliated university, he sought to establish a consistent approach to leadership throughout the university. All the university's stakeholders agreed that leadership was a desired focus, but Dr. Camron knew getting them all to agree on a common leadership approach would be problematic and challenging. He also had to ensure that the chosen leadership approach supported the mission and focus of the school's religious affiliation. Dr. Camron was very aware that selecting the right leadership approach would set the tone for his presidency and could establish a legacy for future generations who attend the university.

President Camron convened a committee from all segments of the campus to research, evaluate, and recommend a leadership approach for the university. Almost immediately, the committee gravitated toward servant leadership. Because theirs is a faith-based university, the committee members recognized the similarities between the mission of the school and the tenets of servant leadership. The servant leadership approach also supported the committee's desire to choose a leadership focus that would empower the university community and was attentive to the concerns of followers and those less fortunate within the local community. Based on the committee's recommendation and President Camron's own vetting of servant leadership with key constituents and trusted friends, the university adopted servant leadership as the leadership approach to emulate throughout the campus.

The campus was quick to embrace the overall concept of servant leadership but was unsure of the expected actions of servant leaders. Realizing this confusion, senior leaders at the university decided to better define the model of servant leadership the university would adopt. President Camron was intrigued by the writings of Robert Greenleaf and Larry Spears (Greenleaf's protégé), and had the senior leaders read both Greenleaf's and Spears's perspectives on servant leadership. He then led a weekend retreat to outline a model of servant leadership for the university based on *Spears's 10 characteristics of servant leadership.*

In implementing this model campus-wide, every student, faculty member, and staff member attended several seminars where the servant leadership model was described and discussed. Each incoming freshman and transfer student underwent a "Servant Academy" to understand servant leadership and to develop strategies to best exemplify and live a life as a servant leader. The university website spotlighted the message that the university was a servant leadership–focused university.

The initial results were very encouraging to President Camron. Students, faculty, and staff began to exemplify the tenets of servant leadership in the classroom and around campus. The trustees of the university were very pleased with the feedback they received from various donors and constituents who visited the campus or interacted with students and faculty. President Camron further exhibited servant leadership tenets through visible actions such as picking up trash at the football stadium after games and volunteering to serve students in the cafeteria. Overall, the first semester of the campus's focus on servant leadership provided a hopeful start.

During the second semester, though, students and faculty seemed to lose focus on being servant leaders. Students were having difficulty understanding some of the *10 characteristics of servant leadership*, expressing their belief that the model was somewhat complicated. A key issue among students was trying to embrace the tenets of servant leadership while simultaneously competing against each other for awards, scholarships, and recognition. Several faculty members used tenets of servant leadership as an excuse for inflating grades and not rewarding the most deserving students. Servant leadership seemed to conflict with the values of students who were achievement-oriented and wanted to excel. The notion of trying to get the highest grade point in the class did not seem to mesh with the altruistic values of servant leadership. Faculty also began to question the

(Continued)

(Continued)

selection of the servant leadership model by only a small group of university leaders. Some administrators found that the model's tenets made it difficult to prioritize tasks and allocate resources to meet the differing needs of the university and community.

President Camron is committed to developing a culture of servant leadership throughout the university as he sees great benefits from the university community having a common purpose and focus on serving others. But he is beginning to have major misgivings about it. He knows the university community is still adjusting to this new focus, but the concerns expressed and the rising resistance to the servant leadership model have made him question whether it will work at his university. Servant leadership is consistent with the school's religious orientation, but is it workable for education?

Questions

1. Was servant leadership an appropriate leadership model for the university to adopt? Explain your answer.

2. Which of the 10 characteristics of servant leadership defined by Spears (2002) do you think created frustration and confusion for the students and faculty?

3. Is it appropriate for an administration to require faculty and students to adopt an entire template of values such as those inherent in servant leadership? Explain your answer.

Advanced Questions

4. Describe a different process President Camron could have used to develop a model of servant leadership for the university.

5. Could a more diverse, public university implement servant leadership as its model of leadership?

6. One of the criticisms of servant leadership is that it is moralistic. What is your personal response to servant leadership and, specifically, President Camron's leadership?

—John Baker, Western Kentucky University

REFERENCES

Ehrhart, M. G. (2004). Leadership and procedural justice climate as antecedents of unit-level organizational citizenship behavior. *Personnel Psychology, 57,* 61–94.

Graham, J. W. (1991). Servant leadership in organizations: Inspirational and moral. *Leadership Quarterly, 2,* 105–119.

Hale, J. R., & Fields, D. L. (2007). Exploring servant leadership across cultures: A study of followers in Ghana and the USA. *Leadership, 3,* 397–417.

Liden, R. C., Panaccio, A., Hu, J., & Meuser, J. D. (2015). Servant leadership: Antecedents, consequences, and contextual moderators. In D. V. Day (Ed.), *The Oxford handbook of leadership and organizations.* Oxford, UK: Oxford University Press.

Northouse, P. G. (2019). *Leadership: Theory and practice* (8th ed.). Thousand Oaks, CA: Sage.

Spears, L. C. (2002). Tracing the past, present, and future of servant-leadership. In L. C. Spears & M. Lawrence (Eds.), *Focus on leadership: Servant-leadership for the 21st century* (pp. 1–16). New York, NY: Wiley.

Spears, L. C. (2010). Servant leadership and Robert K. Greenleaf's legacy. In D. van Dierendonck & K. Patterson (Eds.), *Servant leadership: Developments in theory and research* (pp. 11–24). New York, NY: Palgrave Macmillan.

Walumbwa, F. O., Hartnell, C. A., & Oke, A. (2010). Servant leadership, procedural justice climate, service climate, employee attitudes, and organizational citizenship behavior: A cross-level investigation. *Journal of Applied Psychology, 95,* 517–529.

11

Adaptive Leadership

INTRODUCTION

Perhaps no other field is as uniquely positioned to engage in adaptive leadership as education. Being in education today is like walking up a down escalator—the changes keep coming: funding, technology, governmental standards, parental pressures, standardized testing . . . The list goes on. At the same time, people recognize that education is in a crisis, and changes in how we educate our young people are being demanded. As a result, leadership in education is required at all levels from government education agencies and school administrators to teachers, specialists, parents, and communities, and much of that leadership will be adaptive.

Adaptive leadership is about helping people change and adjust to new situations. While the name of this approach, adaptive leadership, makes one think it is concerned with how leaders adapt, it is actually more about the adaptations of followers. Originally formulated by Heifetz (1994), adaptive leadership conceptualizes the leader not as one who solves problems for people, but rather as one who encourages others to

Figure 11.1 Model of Adaptive Leadership

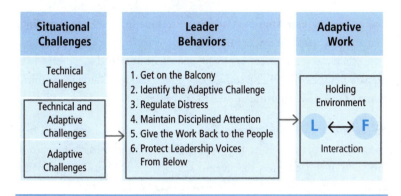

SOURCE: Reprinted from Northouse, P. G., *Leadership: Theory and Practice*, 8th ed. (2019), p. 261, Thousand Oaks, CA: SAGE. Reprinted with permission.

do the problem solving. Adaptive leadership is defined as "the practice of mobilizing people to tackle tough challenges and thrive" (Heifetz, Grashow, & Linsky, 2009, p. 14). Similarly, DeRue (2011) describes adaptive leadership as a process where individuals engage in repeated leading–following interactions that evolve as group needs change, enabling groups to adapt and remain viable in dynamic contexts. Ultimately, adaptive leadership is about leader behaviors that encourage learning, creativity, and adaptation by followers in complex situations.

Figure 11.1 shows a model of the major components of adaptive leadership—*situational challenges*, *leader behaviors*, and *adaptive work*—and how they fit together. Leaders confront three kinds of *situational challenges* (technical, technical and adaptive, and adaptive), but adaptive leadership is concerned with helping people address adaptive challenges. The six *leader behaviors* that play a major role in the process are (1) *get on the balcony*, (2) *identify adaptive challenges*, (3) *regulate distress*, (4) *maintain disciplined attention*, (5) *give the work back to the people*, and (6) *protect leadership voices from below*. These six behaviors form a kind of recipe for being an adaptive leader. *Adaptive work* is the focus and goal of adaptive leadership. Central to adaptive work is *a holding environment*, a space created and maintained by adaptive leaders where people can feel secure as they confront and resolve difficult life challenges.

CASE STUDIES

The following case studies describe situations in educational settings that require adaptive leadership. The first case is about the issues that arise when a teacher offers to pay for a student to attend a conference to prepare her for college. The second case looks at how a student organization at a university must adapt when it loses a majority of its funding.

At the end of each case, you will find two sets of questions that will help in analyzing the case. The first set can be answered using information provided in this chapter; the second set, Advanced Questions, provides an opportunity to analyze the case using ideas from the adaptive leadership perspective and is designed to coincide with the concepts discussed in Chapter 11 of *Leadership: Theory and Practice* (8th ed., pp. 257–292).

CASE 11.1

PRIDE, POLICIES, AND PROMISE

Maria is a high school junior who has achieved an overall 4.0 GPA since entering high school in seventh grade. She attends a rural, public high school that encompasses Grades 7–12. The average class enrollment is just under 100; Maria's class has 93 students. The community she lives in is very poor but extremely close-knit. While everyone seems to know everyone else's business, those living in or near the small town of 3,000 can always count on their neighbors for help when it is needed.

Throughout her life, Maria has watched her parents work hard to make ends meet and provide for their family. Her father works two jobs, and her mother works in the local processing plant. Maria respects and loves her family but wants more than a life of working in a factory or on an assembly line.

Maria has tested in the top fifth percentile of all high school juniors in the country. Based on her test scores, she qualifies to attend a weeklong conference focusing on academic success and preparing students to compete for admission to the best universities and for scholarships. Maria sees the conference as key to her breaking the familial cycle of factory work; however, she does not have the $1,500 tuition fee required to attend the conference.

Mr. Brisbee, the popular high school physics teacher, is considered well-off by those in the community (thanks to an inheritance) and has offered to pay for Maria to attend the conference. Mr. Brisbee made the offer because Maria is extremely bright, has a very promising future in higher education, and reminds him of his niece who died two years earlier from a rare blood disease. Maria is ecstatic at Mr. Brisbee's offer.

(Continued)

(Continued)

When Maria's parents learn of Mr. Brisbee's offer, they are insistent that she decline it. They say that she should not attend the conference if they cannot provide the money to pay for it. Much like other people in their community and the region, Maria's parents are very proud, and while they see Mr. Brisbee's offer as kind, accepting it indicates that they cannot provide for their family.

Maria is distraught. She desperately wants to attend the conference to better prepare herself to compete for acceptance into universities and, more importantly, for scholarships that will allow her to pursue higher education.

Most of Maria's fellow students are supportive of her and understand her desire to accept the gift to attend the conference. A vocal minority of students, however, support Maria's parents and view Maria as a student who thinks she is "too good for our town." They say Maria should obey her parents' wishes and decline Mr. Brisbee's offer.

To further complicate the issue, the school principal has informed Mr. Brisbee that there is a district policy that forbids teachers from providing any favors to students outside of the classroom in order to maintain strong role boundaries between teachers and students. The policy is also there to protect teachers from being accused of having "special" relationships with students.

Other teachers at the high school, however, are very supportive of Maria's attending the conference, saying she is a great role model for other students at the high school. The teachers formed an informal group to accomplish two things: They've asked the school board to revise the policy so that Mr. Brisbee's gift to Maria is considered a "scholarship" and, if that's adopted, to then develop strategies to help influence Maria's parents to change their minds. The school board is divided: Half its members support the teachers' group request; the other half say the policy should stand.

As the deadline for registering for the conference nears, Maria is afraid there will be no chance to change her parents' minds and make her dreams a reality.

Questions

1. Adaptive leadership is about mobilizing people to embrace needed change. In this case, who are the people who need to think about change? What changes do they need to make? Who are the people (adaptive leaders) who will mobilize this change?

2. Is there a technical "fix" for the challenges people face in this case? Would a technical solution be effective for everyone involved? Discuss.

3. Adaptive leadership usually requires that people reexamine their personal values regarding an issue. What values do Maria, her parents, the teachers, the students, the board, Mr. Brisbee, and the principal have to reexamine?

Advanced Questions

4. If you were a school board member who supported Maria and Mr. Brisbee, how would you go about creating a place or situation (holding environment) in which these issues could be discussed?

5. Imagine you are the principal of Maria's school. Citing examples, explain how you could *give the work back to the people* and *protect leadership voices from below.*

6. Considering the complexity involved in Maria's request, do you think adaptive leadership would be workable in this situation? Defend your answer.

—John Baker, Western Kentucky University

CASE 11.2

SAVING SAVE THE WHALES AND SEALS

Josiah is the president of Save the Whales and Seals (SWS), a registered student organization at State University. The group is one of the largest and most respected on the public university's campus. SWS is best known for its numerous and successful Alternative Break service trips to coastal areas, where members engage in volunteer work with local community organizations to improve the health of the ocean and its wildlife. This past academic year, SWS coordinated 10 trips over Winter Break, 35 during Spring Break, and another 10 in May at the end of the academic year. One of the reasons SWS has enjoyed success is because of its close and supportive relationship with State University's Student Activities (SA) Office, which provides significant funding and logistical planning help. Members interested in participating on a trip are only required to submit a deposit of $20 to reserve a spot and to attend an orientation session prior to the trip.

Like many public colleges in the United States, State University has experienced significant decreases in its funding from its state government. The university is not willing to make cuts to its academic programs, so co-curricular departments, particularly the SA Office, have been particularly hard hit. The SA Office has been forced to make the difficult decision to sever its funding to SWS, a decision that is potentially catastrophic for the organization.

Josiah and the club's treasurer, Sandra, have determined that for each service trip to occur, the group needs to raise more than $10,000 to cover costs for transportation, housing, insurance, and supplies. Overall, SWS will need to raise more than $500,000 to continue at its current level of volunteering. While Josiah knows that raising the cost of individual participation is an option, increasing it to the level required to substitute for previous university support means each student would pay more than $1,000 per trip. Moreover, he knows that a significant amount of work will be required to train SWS members to plan the logistics of each trip.

To continue its work, Josiah believes SWS must become, in part, a fund-raising organization. However, he knows that its members have not joined SWS motivated to raise money; several of them have made comments that they believe groups that engage in such behavior often become nothing more than salespeople interested in easy ways to make money. Such comments have caused him to fear that the university's decision to cut funding may subsequently tear the organization apart.

Worried about SWS's future, Josiah has brought the organization's small executive board together for a meeting on how to address these issues with the larger SWS membership. The board members had previously discussed the potential for losing university support, and Josiah knows he can rely on them to help explain the situation to other members and move the organization forward.

After discussing various reactions they can expect from SWS members, the board members have developed a plan: In the next general meeting of the group, they will outline the specific issues now facing SWS, and their consideration of these. They will elicit feedback and ideas from SWS members by breaking out into small discussion groups led by board members. Each small group will culminate in the creation of proposals for fund-raising efforts that might involve both individual initiatives and group collaboration.

Josiah then leads the board members in brainstorming ideas on how they will deal with group members expressing extreme resistance to the shift to fund-raising activities, allowing these members to express their thoughts and feelings without letting the meeting devolve into a grumbling session. The board concludes its meeting by scheduling a follow-up meeting to

(Continued)

(Continued)

occur after the general session, where the board members will focus on ways to maintain momentum and continue progress in their plan to restructure how SWS successfully conducts its service work.

Questions

1. Which aspects of the case are examples of technical challenges, and which are adaptive challenges?

2. How can Josiah and the executive board frame the message of the need to change in a way that reduces the group's tendency to view the problem as a technical issue and increase its ability to think adaptively?

3. What are some specific examples of how Josiah and the executive board have attempted to get on the balcony? What other actions could they take to better see the big picture of what is occurring within SWS?

Advanced Questions

4. Given the board's plan, how can its members effectively provide a holding environment within their planned meeting to allow adaptive work to occur?

5. After the meeting has occurred, what could Josiah and other board members do to maintain disciplined attention on the need to fund-raise and ensure that group members are not simply looking for the executive board to solve the issue?

6. Central to adaptive leadership is the idea that people (followers) have to be mobilized to deal with change. Do you think the students in this case are going to be willing to change their perceptions and attitudes about SWS and engage in fund-raising? Defend your answer.

*—David Rosch, University of Illinois
at Urbana-Champaign*

REFERENCES

DeRue, D. S. (2011). Adaptive leadership theory: Leading and following as a complex adaptive process. *Research in Organizational Behavior, 31*, 125–150.

Heifetz, R. A. (1994). *Leadership without easy answers.* Cambridge, MA: Belknap Press.

Heifetz, R. A., Grashow, A., & Linsky, M. (2009). *The practice of adaptive leadership: Tools and tactics for changing your organization and the world.* Boston, MA: Harvard Business School Press.

Northouse, P. G. (2019). *Leadership: Theory and practice* (8th ed.). Thousand Oaks, CA: SAGE.

12

Followership

We exist in a leader-centric world. The field of education, with teachers, faculty, administrators, and others in roles of authority and influence, is particularly focused on the "leader" of leadership, with relatively little attention paid to followers. But leadership is a *shared process* involving the interdependence between leaders and followers in a shared relationship. Followers are an integral part of that relationship. Without followers, there would be no leaders.

Understanding the roles and impacts that followers play in the leadership process is the focus of the study of followership. Followership is defined as "*a process whereby an individual or individuals accept the influence of others to accomplish a common goal*" (Northouse, 2019, p. 295). Followership involves a power differential between the follower and the leader. Typically, followers comply with the directions and wishes of leaders—they defer to leaders' power. Through these interactions, followers have an impact on the leader and organizational outcomes.

Followership can be divided into two broad categories: *role-based* and *relational-based* (Uhl-Bien, Riggio, Lowe, & Carsten, 2014). The *role-based* perspective focuses on followers in regard to the typical roles or behaviors they exhibit while occupying a formal or informal position within a hierarchical system. Emphasis in the role-based perspective is on the roles and styles of followers and how their behaviors affect the leader and organizational outcomes.

The *relational-based* system of followership is tied to *interpersonal behaviors* rather than specific roles, focusing on one person's attempt to influence and the other person's response to these influence attempts (DeRue & Ashford, 2010; Fairhurst & Uhl-Bien, 2012; Uhl-Bien et al., 2014). The *relational-based* approach is based on social constructivism, a sociological theory that argues that people create meaning about their reality as they interact with each other.

As there are many types of leaders, so, too, are there many types of followers. Grouping followers' roles into distinguishable categories to create a typology of follower behaviors has been undertaken by several researchers (Chaleff, 1995; Kellerman, 2008; Kelley, 1992; Zaleznik, 1965). Typologies provide characterizations of individuals engaged in the followership process that can assist leaders in effectively communicating with followers. By knowing that a follower adheres to a certain type of behavior, the leader can adapt her or his style to optimally relate to the role the follower is playing.

As you can see in Table 12.1, there are distinct differences in characterizations of followers in these different typologies, but there are also some commonalities. Generally, the major types of followers are active–engaged, independent–assertive, submissive–compliant, and supportive–conformer—or, as suggested by Carsten et al. (2014), passive followers, anti-authoritarian followers, and proactive followers.

Followers can have positive and negative impacts on an organization. Carsten et al. (2014) identified several positive facets, or perspectives, of followership and the impact followers can have on an organization. They found that followers *get the job done, work in the best interest of the organization's mission, challenge leaders, support the leader,* and *learn from leaders.*

Table 12.1 Typologies of Followership

Zaleznik (1965)	Kelley (1992)	Chaleff (1995)	Kellerman (2008)
Withdrawn	Alienated	Resource	Isolate
Masochistic	Passive	Individualist	Bystander
Compulsive	Conformist	Implementer	Participant
Impulsive	Pragmatist	Partner	Activist
	Exemplary		Diehard

SOURCE: Adapted from Crossman, B., & Crossman, J. (2011). Conceptualizing followership: A review of the literature. *Leadership, 7*(4), 481–497.

In addition to having a positive impact, there is a dark side to follower-ship. Lipman-Blumen (2005) identified a series of psychological factors of followers that can lead to followers engaging in ineffective, and even harmful, roles that allow destructive leadership to flourish. These factors include people's *need for reassuring authority figures*; *need for security and certainty*; *need to feel chosen or special*; *need for membership in the human community*; *fear of ostracism, isolation, and social death*; and *fear of power-lessness to challenge a bad leader*. When followers attempt to fulfill these needs or give into their fears, it can create contexts where unethical and destructive leaders can thrive.

CASE STUDIES

The following case studies describe situations in educational settings in which servant leadership is present. The first case looks at how follower-ship helped revamp a dysfunctional high school robotics team. The sec-ond case examines a university's efforts to adopt a servant leadership model for its campus.

At the end of each case, you will find two sets of questions that will help in analyzing the case. The first set can be answered using informa-tion provided in this chapter; the second set, Advanced Questions, provides an opportunity to analyze the case using ideas from the servant leadership perspective and is designed to coincide with the concepts discussed in Chapter 12 of *Leadership: Theory and Practice* (8th ed., pp. 293–334).

CASE 12.1

REVAMPING THE ROBOTICS TEAM

Ross Dumont coaches a high school robotics team at an urban high school. The team is composed of students who design, build, and program a robot to compete at an annual state competition. At the initial team meeting each year, at least 20 interested students show up, but as the semester goes on, fewer and fewer come. In the past two years the team, which would optimally have 15 members, has only had six. As a result, there are not enough hands to adequately design, build, and program a robot, and the team's robot has done dismally in competition. In addition, the four-year grant a local manufacturing company provided the school to fund the robotics team will run out this year. If the team can do well at the state competition, the company that funded the grant could probably be convinced to continue it, but the company's leaders are as disappointed as Mr. Dumont is in how badly the team has performed.

At the robotics team's first meeting of the new school year, there are 17 interested students, including four seniors who have been with the team since it started. But Mr. Dumont tells the group that the past poor attendance by team members, the bad performance of the team at competition, and the possibility of losing the grant funding make him believe this will be the last year for the team. He says only the students who can commit to attending all the team meetings should sign up. As a result, only a handful do, and the students leave the meeting feeling as dispirited as Mr. Dumont.

As the meeting is breaking up, however, one of the returning students, Marshawn Johnson, approaches Mr. Dumont. Marshawn angrily tells Mr. Dumont that if no one shows up to be on the team, it is the coach's fault because all his speech did was discourage kids from participating. Marshawn says Mr. Dumont is an incompetent coach who could

(Continued)

care less about what the students want or need and plays favorites with the team members, which is why students don't stick with the team. "If you don't want to coach the team anymore, then say so," Marshawn says, "and let us find another adviser." Mr. Dumont is stunned and looks around the room at other students, to see if others concur, but most of them turn away or avoid eye contact.

The next day in the hallway, Mr. Dumont sees three of the team's other returning students—Andre, Alexis, and Benita—and asks them if they have a minute to talk. They look warily at each other and step into Mr. Dumont's room. Before Mr. Dumont can say anything, Andre speaks up. "If this is about what Marshawn said yesterday, I don't want to be part of it," he says. "I just want the team to continue because I need it on my college applications."

Mr. Dumont looks at Alexis. "What about you?" She shrugs. "I don't think you are a bad coach," she says. "I'm allowed to work on the parts of the project I want to work on."

He turns to Benita. "And you?" Benita hesitates, thinking for a moment. Then she speaks. She explains that because the team is a club activity that meets in the evenings, transportation is a problem for most of the kids who rely on bus transportation to school and come from families where one or both parents work nights. Because Mr. Dumont sets the team's meeting schedule, these students don't feel like they have any choice in the matter. As for playing favorites, Benita says it does seem as if Mr. Dumont is partial to the kids who show up consistently, but she can understand that. Finally, she suggests he meet with the other students who have been part of the team before and ask for their ideas for improvement.

The meeting is held and a lot of issues are brought up, but in the end Mr. Dumont realizes that Benita was right about the evening meetings being problematic for students. Mr. Dumont learns that most of the team's members would prefer to meet on Saturdays and have one long workday together. As for the work that needs to be done between those meetings, the students suggest splitting the team up into three groups: designers, builders, and programmers, with captains for each group. The captains and Mr. Dumont can meet weekly to coordinate each group's work plans. It's decided that Marshawn, Andre, and Benita will be the captains because they can all meet during the same lunch period with Mr. Dumont. The captains are then charged with arranging meeting schedules for their own groups, and Benita suggests that these meetings be held in the students' neighborhoods, rather than at school. Alexis suggests the groups use video or audio calls to communicate with one another during the week.

Because he is used to supervising all aspects of the robotics team, Mr. Dumont isn't sure how well these new arrangements will work. To his surprise, however, the weekly captains' meetings are very productive and, when the team members come to the Saturday workdays, they are focused and prepared. Mr. Dumont notices that during captains' meetings, Marshawn is reticent to admit when his group is having challenges, but the other captains push him to talk openly about those challenges because his group's work affects the other groups' progress.

The state competition is a month away, and Mr. Dumont is shocked. The team's robot is designed, built, programmed, and in testing. The groups no longer have regular weekly meetings; the Saturday work sessions provide sufficient time for the team to test the robot and make any needed changes to its operation. Mr. Dumont is so happy with the progress that he invites the representatives from the manufacturing company funding the team to come and observe one of the Saturday sessions. The engineers from the company have some suggestions to which the students are receptive. Before he leaves, the company's lead engineer remarks to the students that he wished his own engineering teams were as well coordinated and committed to the group success as theirs are.

Questions

1. Which of the typologies identified in Table 12.1 best characterizes the roles Marshawn, Andre, Benita, and Alexis play on the robotics team?

2. Would you say the followership on the team is role-based or relational-based? Explain your answer.

(Continued)

(Continued)

3. It appears the robotics team is going to have a better year than in the past. Why is that so? Is it the result of leadership or followership? How do the actions and attitudes of Mr. Dumont and Marshawn play into what has happened? Discuss.

Advanced Questions

4. Using the criteria identified in the new perspectives of followership (*getting the job done, challenging leaders*, etc.), how would you evaluate each of the people in the case?

5. Reversing the lens emphasizes that followers can be change agents—what was the impact of followers' characteristics on followers' behaviors in this case?

6. Do you think Mr. Dumont was a bad leader? Using Lipman-Blumen's psychological factors and dysfunctional leadership, discuss why students who thought so might have continued on the team.

—Authors

CHOOSING A CHAIR

The chair of the Political Science Department, Joe Hussein, died suddenly from a heart attack, and the dean needs to put a new chair in place quickly as the department is in the midst of an arduous accreditation process that Joe was leading.

The dean feels there are five candidates on the department's faculty who might fill the role, and asks the department's administrative assistant, Donna Russell, to meet with him to help vet who would be the best of these candidates to fill the gap. The dean worked with Donna in another department before she transferred to Political Science and knows Donna was Joe's right-hand person and because of that has unique insight into the faculty and staff of the Poli Sci Department.

The five faculty the dean discusses with Donna are

- Mark Andrews, who has been in the department for 22 years. Mark has the most seniority and certainly knows the department well, although he takes a very low profile in the department and seldom goes to any faculty social events. He attends faculty meetings, but rarely makes any comments. He has participated on prior accreditation teams and is serving on the current one as well. Donna reports that while Mark is very knowledgeable, his participation on the accreditation team is limited to providing advice and statements like "This is the way we did this last time." Unlike other team members, he does not volunteer to do any extra work involved in writing the accreditation reports.

- Kathy Dorn, who was turned down for the chair's job the last time it was open. Kathy told Donna that she believes she didn't get the job because she is a woman. Donna says, however, that Joe told her that Kathy was denied the chair's job because other faculty

(Continued)

don't like working with her, stating that she is petty and vindictive. Kathy has strong administrative skills and seems to enjoy the prestige that comes along with having power. She is the adviser for the undergraduates and has been known to say bad things about her colleagues, including the department's chair, to students.

- Corrine O'Brien, who has only been a faculty member for five years, but has gained a lot of attention for her work in environmental politics. She has brought in multiple, multiyear grants and was recently appointed to an advisory board for the Environmental Protection Agency. Corrine has a reputation for advocacy and has met multiple times with the university's president to discuss the institution's sustainability practices. Donna says Corrine, who is also on the accreditation team, has brought energy and focus to the team's efforts and happily volunteers to take on extra work. Some people dislike Corrine because she seems driven and too research oriented. Donna greatly respects Corrine, but feels she may be too busy to take on the chair's role.

- Marius Donovan, who Donna describes as a "quiet giant." Not outspoken, Marius is liked by everyone and seen as the "bedrock" of the department. He was the one who aggressively recruited Corrine to come to the university and suggested many of the changes that Joe put in place to make the department run more smoothly. Marius, however, is introverted and greatly dislikes confrontation. He overheard Kathy Dorn tell a student not to enroll in one of his courses because "it was outdated and trivial" and chose not to address it with her.

- Benjamin Torres is a popular teacher and well-regarded researcher in the field of state politics. He is often interviewed by the news media about state politics, which some of the other faculty think makes him a bit arrogant. As evidence of his arrogance, Donna (who admits she butts heads with Benjamin now and then) says that Benjamin was never afraid to question Joe about department issues, even in front of other faculty members. She says that didn't seem to affect Joe and Ben's relationship; they were running partners who worked out together nearly every day. She knows that Joe often talked departmental business with Ben on those runs, but whatever was said stayed between them.

Questions

1. Donna Russell is in a good position to observe different faculty members. Her observations seem directly related to how well each faculty member plays the follower role. Does it make sense to use *followership* as a criterion for selecting the chair (*leadership*)? Explain your answer.

2. Which of the typologies identified in Table 12.1 most accurately describe the different roles the faculty members play? Which individuals would you characterize as being passive followers, anti-authoritarian followers, or proactive followers?

3. Using the roles identified in Chaleff's follower typology, what roles do each of the faculty members the dean is considering play in the department?

Advanced Questions

4. Using the criteria identified in the new perspectives of followership (*getting the job done, challenging leaders*, etc.), how would you evaluate each of these faculty members?

5. By job description, Donna is an administrative assistant, or follower, in the department, yet she seems to have power and exerts leadership. How do *leading* and *following* get played out in Donna's work? Based on your observations of Donna's work in the department, what is more important—leadership or followership?

6. Unhealthy followership occurs as a result of people's needs to find safety, feel unique, and be included in community. Using Lipman-Blumen's psychological factors and dysfunctional leadership, discuss how the faculty described above might engage in negative followership behaviors.

—Authors

REFERENCES

Carsten, M. K., Harms, P., & Uhl-Bien, M. (2014). Exploring historical perspectives of followership: The need for an expanded view of followers and follower role. In L. M. Lapierre & M. K. Carsten (Eds.), *Followership: What is it and why do people follow?* (pp. 3–25). Bingley, UK: Emerald Group.

Chaleff, I. (1995). *The courageous follower: Standing up to and for our leaders* (3rd ed.). San Francisco, CA: Berrett-Koehler.

Crossman, B., & Crossman, J. (2011). Conceptualizing followership: A review of the literature. *Leadership, 7*(4), 481–497.

DeRue, S., & Ashford, S. (2010). Who will lead and who will follow? A social process of leadership identity construction in organizations. *Academy of Management Review, 35*(4), 627–647.

Fairhurst, G. T., & Uhl-Bien, M. (2012). Organizational discourse analysis (ODA): Examining leadership as a relational process. *The Leadership Quarterly, 23*(6), 1043–1062.

Kellerman, B. (2008). *Followership: How followers are creating change and changing leaders.* Boston, MA: Harvard Business Press.

Kelley, R. E. (1992). *The power of followership.* New York, NY: Doubleday Business.

Lipman-Blumen, J. (2005). *The allure of toxic leaders: Why we follow destructive bosses and corrupt politicians—and how we can survive them.* New York, NY: Oxford University Press.

Northouse, P. G. (2019). *Leadership: Theory and practice* (8th ed.). Thousand Oaks, CA: SAGE.

Uhl-Bien, M., Riggio, R. E., Lowe, K. B., & Carsten, M. K. (2014). Followership theory: A review and research agenda. *Leadership Quarterly, 25*, 83–104.

Zaleznik, A. (1965, May/June). The dynamics of subordinacy. *Harvard Business Review*, p. 118.

13

Leadership Ethics

INTRODUCTION

When we hear about instances of grade inflation, social promotion, falsifying assessment scores, and embezzlement, we cringe. These are all instances where a decision has been made in an educational setting that has strong ethical implications. And as educators, many of us in public schools paid for by tax dollars, public expectations of our ethical behavior is high, not to mention our own personal ethical aspirations.

Ethics is concerned with the kinds of values and morals an individual or a society finds desirable or appropriate. The word *ethics* has its roots in the Greek word *ethos*, which translates to "customs, conduct, or character." When you apply an ethical lens to leadership, you are examining *what leaders do and who leaders are.*

Leadership ethics is concerned with the nature of leaders' behavior, and with their virtuousness. Because leadership involves influence and leaders often have more power than followers, they have an enormous ethical responsibility for how they affect other people. Leaders need to engage followers to accomplish mutual goals; therefore, it is imperative that they treat followers and their ideas with respect and dignity. Leaders also play a major role in establishing the ethical climate in their organizations; that role requires leaders to be particularly sensitive to the values and ideals they promote.

Ethical theory provides a system of rules or principles that guide us in making decisions about what is right or wrong and good or bad in a particular situation. In the Western tradition, ethical theories typically are divided into two kinds: theories about *conduct* and theories about *character*. Theories about conduct emphasize the consequences of leader behavior (teleological approach) or the rules that govern leader behavior (deontological approach). Virtue-based theories focus on the character of leaders, and they stress qualities such as courage, honesty, fairness, and fidelity.

Leaders' choices are also influenced by their moral development. The most widely recognized theory advanced to explain how people think about moral issues is Kohlberg's stages of moral development. Kohlberg (1984) created a classification of moral reasoning that was divided into six stages: *Stage 1—Obedience and Punishment*, *Stage 2—Individualism and Exchange*, *Stage 3—Interpersonal Accord and Conformity*, *Stage 4—Maintaining the Social Order*, *Stage 5—Social Contract and Individual Rights*, and *Stage 6—Universal Principles* (Table 13.1). Kohlberg further classified the first two stages as preconventional morality, the second two as conventional morality, and the last two as postconventional morality.

In addition, there are five recognized principles of ethical leadership, the origins of which can be traced back to Aristotle. Although not inclusive, these principles provide a foundation for the development of sound ethical leadership:

1. *Respect.* Ethical leaders treat others with respect—listening to them closely and being tolerant of opposing points of view.

2. *Service.* Ethical leaders serve others by being altruistic, placing others' welfare ahead of their own in an effort to contribute to the common good.

TABLE 13.1 Kohlberg's Stages of Moral Development

LEVEL 1: PRECONVENTIONAL MORALITY	
Reasoning based on self-interest, avoiding punishment, and rewards	
STAGE 1	**STAGE 2**
Obedience and Punishment	**Individualism and Exchange**
"I follow the rules so I don't get hurt"	*"I will do a favor for you, if you do one for me"*

↓

LEVEL 2: CONVENTIONAL MORALITY	
Reasoning based on society's views and expectations	
STAGE 3	**STAGE 4**
Interpersonal Accord and Conformity	**Maintaining the Social Order**
"I try to be good and do what others expect of me"	*"I follow the rules and support the laws of society"*

↓

LEVEL 3: POSTCONVENTIONAL MORALITY	
Reasoning based on conscience and creating a just society	
STAGE 5	**STAGE 6**
Social Contract and Individual Rights	**Universal Principles**
"I work with others to do what is best for all of us"	*"I act out of my internalized and universal principle of justice"*

SOURCE: Reprinted from "Leadership Ethics" in Northouse, P. G., *Leadership: Theory and Practice,* 8th ed. (2019), p. 337, Thousand Oaks, CA: SAGE. Reprinted with permission.

3. *Justice.* Ethical leaders place fairness at the center of their decision making, including the challenging task of being fair to the individual while simultaneously being fair to the common interests of the community.

4. *Honesty.* Ethical leaders do not lie, nor do they present truth to others in ways that are destructive or counterproductive.

5. *Community.* Ethical leaders are committed to building community, which includes searching for goals that are compatible with the goals of followers and with society as a whole.

The bottom line is that leadership involves values, and one cannot be a leader without being aware of and concerned about one's own values. Because leadership has a moral dimension, being a leader demands awareness on our part of the way our ethics defines our leadership. To be an ethical leader, we must be sensitive to the needs of others, treat others in ways that are just, and care for others.

CASE STUDIES

The following case studies involve ethical leadership decisions in educational settings. The first case describes a high school principal who is asked to give special attention to hiring a young teacher. In the second case, a college department chair asks an instructor to consider changing a student's failing grade.

At the end of each case, you will find two sets of questions that will help in analyzing the case. The first set can be answered using information provided in this chapter; the second set, Advanced Questions, provides an opportunity to analyze the case using ideas from the perspective of leadership ethics and is designed to coincide with the concepts discussed in Chapter 13 of *Leadership: Theory and Practice* (8th ed., pp. 335–370).

CASE 13.1

PLEASE CONSIDER MY DAUGHTER

The Blue Ribbon School District (BRSD) is a well-respected and desirable place to find employment. Ten years ago, the public school district found itself on the losing end of a federal unfair labor practice lawsuit. After the outcome of the case, the district adopted two new hiring policies. The first created an interview protocol including a six-member committee for each new position that comprises at least one parent, one teacher, one staff member, and one administrator. The school board also sends an impartial member to serve on the committee. The committee screens and interviews applicants based on a clear set of agreed-upon criteria and then recommends the two top-ranked candidates to the board. The board is required to follow the ranked order of the recommendations provided by the hiring committee or reopen the position for additional applicants. The second policy involves a public role-call vote for each new hire.

The BRSD is currently in the midst of a multimillion-dollar renovation of its secondary school complex. John Starsley, the principal, and Kelsey Halston, the athletic director, are in constant communication with the construction manager, Joe Warsman. The project was slated as a 20-month project and has 3 months remaining. John and Kelsey have managed most of the headaches from the projects and communicate weekly with Joe. All three feel the project has been a great success, and communication has been open and honest.

Recently, Joe's daughter, Shelly Warsman, graduated from college with a secondary science teaching degree with a minor in recreation education, and wants to work in the BRSD. Coincidentally, the BRSD just posted an opening for a middle school science teaching position and will conduct interviews early next month and hire the following month. Joe, wanting to see his daughter be given an opportunity to be hired, approaches Kelsey to discuss the teaching position, pointing

(Continued)

out that Shelly could also help the school by coaching field hockey. Joe raves about Shelly's outstanding achievements in high school and college, says he knows that Shelly would be an asset to the school, and adds that he would appreciate Kelsey's help with getting her an interview. Kelsey explains the two board policies to Joe and emphasizes that there is nothing she can do to help. Kelsey encourages Joe to have Shelly apply and then allow the hiring process to take place.

Joe, wanting so much to help his daughter obtain her dream job, calls John to set up a private meeting at a restaurant out of the area. John, thinking the meeting is about the construction project, agrees. In the meantime, John has already assembled the interviewing committee for the science teaching position and set dates for the review of all applications. He is encouraged by the number of candidates in the applicant pool who are of high quality and already have several years of experience.

At the lunch meeting, Joe and John's conversation starts off in the normal tone and with the normal type of discourse. After a few minutes, though, Joe starts to frame a scenario. "John, you know how important our children are to us in life. All parents want for their children is for them to be successful and see their dreams fulfilled," he says. After a thoughtful pause, he adds, "My daughter Shelly has applied for your science teaching vacancy. Not only is she a great teacher, but she can be a huge asset to the field hockey program. I am aware of the board policies on hiring, but I also know you have great influence on the outcome of potential employees. As you know, in the construction of the new building, I have made many changes that were not in the contract without charge and helped you and Kelsey save a lot of money, which makes you look good to your board. It is only fair that you give my daughter very serious consideration."

John is caught off guard by Joe's request. "Joe, I am taken back by your attempt to exploit our working relationship in this manner. You are asking me to 'stack the deck,' and I am really not comfortable doing so," John replies.

"You know it is unlike me to ask such a favor, but I am at my wit's end," Joe says. "My wife was most recently diagnosed with advanced cancer, and she so wants to see my daughter succeed. I know you are still over budget on the building project, so I am more than willing to continue to help you and Kelsey trim costs by using materials that may not be up to code but would be adequate for the school."

"Joe, I am so sorry to hear about your wife," John says. "You know I lost my mother last year to cancer, and it is a hard thing. But to even consider this is a huge gamble for me. If anyone found out, I would be risking everything."

Joe assures John that the school project would be completed under budget and that he would make sure the school passes all building inspections. All he wants from John is that his daughter be given special consideration for the new teaching position.

Questions

1. If John decides to move forward and help Joe's daughter, what are the possible risks? What could the rewards be?

2. Where are John and Joe on Kohlberg's stages of moral development?

3. Applying the five principles of ethical leadership, outline exactly how John should approach the proposal by Joe in each of the five areas.

Advanced Questions

4. Using the three different theories of making decisions based on moral conduct (ethical egoism, utilitarianism, and altruism), explain the impact to other people of John's decision.

5. Could this situation be an example of the dark side of leadership? Explain your answer.

6. If Shelly is hired and proves to be an outstanding teacher and state title–winning field hockey coach, could it be argued that the decision was an ethical one? Defend your answer.

—Thomas Starmack, Bloomsburg University

"CUT HER SOME SLACK"

It is the last morning of finals week, and Dr. Alex Morgan, the department chair, is having a cup of coffee while casually reviewing the list of his department's graduating students and their final grades. He is checking to see if any students who have applied for graduation have encountered an issue that will keep them from being part of the ceremony. Usually it is outstanding library or parking fines that need to be resolved, but occasionally there's a case where a student has failed a course in his or her last semester and does not have enough credits to graduate.

Alex almost spits out his coffee when he sees one of the department's international students on the list: Mimi, a student from Malaysia. Ever since Dr. Morgan had Mimi in class when she was a freshman, he has had a soft spot for her. As she is the first member of her family to go to college, Mimi's parents, who work in menial civil servant jobs, saved and scrimped for years to be able to send their only child to the United States for school. Their future is tightly wrapped up in Mimi's ability to get a good job and support them as they age.

Dr. Morgan has been a mentor to Mimi over the years, helping her to navigate the cultural and language differences she's experienced. He is looking forward to meeting her parents when they arrive the next day from Malaysia. Mimi's parents are so grateful to Dr. Morgan for his kindness to their daughter that they wrote to him two months ago asking if they could take him out for a celebratory dinner after the graduation ceremony.

Alex immediately calls Davis Alvarez, the adjunct instructor who teaches the course Mimi has failed. Davis has taught the senior-level course for two years now, and Alex considered getting him to teach as a victory for the department. Davis is recognized as an expert in his field, and the students rave about how much they learn from him.

When asked about Mimi's grade, Davis explains that Mimi's work in the class was not good enough to pass. "She had an extremely hard time grasping the concepts, and the weekly papers she was required to write were very badly done," he says. "In addition, the members of her group all turned in evaluations of her that said she didn't participate in group meetings, and they had to rewrite her portion of the group paper.

"I am not sure how she got this far in school," Davis adds. "Her English is horrible; you can't understand what she's saying when she talks, and her writing is even worse. She relied heavily on spell check and didn't know when it gave her incorrect words. She doesn't speak in class, and I would often see her looking at her phone while I was lecturing and assumed she was checking Facebook or texting."

Alex tells Davis that he is being a little harsh. Alex has watched Mimi develop from a shy freshman with language difficulties to someone he feels he can converse with in English fairly easily. He explains that Mimi's reticence in class is based on her cultural values, and when she is looking at her phone during lectures, it's because she is using a translation app to look up words the instructor is using that she is unfamiliar with.

"Alex, you asked me to teach this class because of my professional background and its value to preparing our students for the real world. I take that role very, very seriously," Davis responds. "I don't want these students to go out into the working world without the right preparation. Mimi will not make it out there. You put her in a job, and she will fail because she doesn't have the skills she needs. Not only would that reflect badly on this college, but it would reflect badly on me."

Alex tells Davis how hard Mimi has tried and how important it is to her and her family that she graduate. "Her family can't afford to send her to school for another semester," Alex explains. "They actually took out a loan so they could fly here to see her get her diploma Saturday. She is going to return to Malaysia to work and

(Continued)

(Continued)

not stay in the United States. She will be fine in her own country where there are not the language difficulties."

Davis is unmoved. "International students come to the United States to be educated to U.S. standards. I don't think they should receive any special accommodations because they are from a foreign country. We don't go easy on our American students if their English is awful and they can't write. We flunk them and make them try again."

Alex spends another 10 minutes trying to get Davis to be more sympathetic to Mimi's dilemma, concluding with "C'mon, Davis, lighten up a little and cut her some slack. At a minimum, give her a C so she can graduate. Giving her a C will not hurt anyone and will help her family a lot."

Davis is quiet for a moment and then responds, "Alex, I am not changing her grade. She didn't do the work, and she doesn't deserve to pass. I am sorry her parents will come halfway across the world only to find out she didn't graduate. But I am not compromising my standards.

"If you don't like my standards, then don't ask me to teach again," he says.

Questions

1. Based on the five characteristics of ethical leadership, describe the ethical behavior of both Alex and Davis.

2. Where would you place Alex and Davis on Kohlberg's stages of moral development? Explain your answer.

3. As Department Chair, Alex has access to the records and could change Mimi's grade himself. What are the possible consequences, positive and negative, if he does so? Does one of these outweigh the others?

Advanced Questions

4. Using the three different theories of making decisions based on moral conduct (ethical egoism, utilitarianism, and altruism), describe how both Alex and Davis see their positions as ethical.

5. Describe how each of the principles of distributive justice can be applied to Mimi's case.

6. Is there a compromise that can be made to resolve the situation that would be ethical? Explain your answer.

—Authors

REFERENCES

Kohlberg, L. (1984). *Essays on moral development: The psychology of moral development* (Vol. 2). New York, NY: Harper & Row.

Northouse, P. G. (2019). *Leadership: Theory and practice* (8th ed.). Thousand Oaks, CA: SAGE.

14

Team Leadership

INTRODUCTION

In today's world, the power of one isn't enough anymore. To get more done with fewer resources, bring together far-flung followers, and harness the collective energy of many minds, organizations establish teams. Education is no different, and in fact has probably employed team leadership longer than many other disciplines.

If you have ever been part of a senior executive team, project management team, task force, work unit, standing committee, quality team, or improvement team, then you've experienced team leadership. Susan E. Kogler Hill, who wrote the invited chapter on the team leadership approach in *Leadership: Theory and Practice* (8th ed.), defines a team as "a type of organizational group that is composed of members who are interdependent, who share common goals, and who must coordinate their activities to accomplish these goals" (Hill, 2019, p. 371). In addition, she notes that teams can be located in the same place meeting face-to-face, or they can be geographically dispersed "virtual" teams meeting via various forms of communication technology.

The organizational team-based structure is an important way for organizations to be able to respond quickly and adapt to constant, rapid changes. Effective organizational teams lead to many desirable outcomes, such as

- greater productivity,

- more effective use of resources,

- better decisions and problem solving,

- better-quality products and services, and

- greater innovation and creativity (Parker, 1990).

The increased importance of organizational teams and the leadership needed for them has produced a growing interest in team leadership theory. The ideas of "team leadership" are quite different from leadership within the organizational vertical structure because they are very *process oriented*. The critical function of a team leader is to help the team accomplish its goals by monitoring and diagnosing the team and taking the necessary actions.

The Hill Model for Team Leadership (Figure 14.1) shows the various decisions team leaders must make to improve a team's effectiveness. In order to determine what actions to take, a leader needs to decide:

1. What type of intervention should be used, *monitoring* or *action taking*?

2. Should the intervention be targeted at an *internal level* or an *external level*?

3. What *leadership actions* should be implemented to improve team functioning?

Hill's model portrays leadership as a team oversight function in which the leader's role is to do whatever is necessary to help the team achieve effectiveness. However, both team leaders and team members can use the model to make decisions about the current functioning of their team and the specific actions they need to take, if any, to improve the team's functioning.

Figure 14.1 The Hill Model for Team Leadership

Leadership Decisions
Monitor or Take Action
Task or Relational
Internal or External

Internal Leadership Actions   **External Leadership Actions**

Task	**Relational**	**Environmental**
Goal Focusing	Coaching	Networking
Structuring for Results	Collaborating	Advocating
Facilitating Decisions	Managing Conflict	Negotiating Support
Training	Building Commitment	Buffering Assessing
Maintaining Standards	Satisfying Needs	Sharing Information
	Modeling Principles	

Team Effectiveness
Performance
Development

SOURCE: Reprinted from "Team Leadership" by S. E. K. Hill in Northouse, P. G., *Leadership: Theory and Practice,* 8th ed. (2019), p. 374, Thousand Oaks, CA: SAGE. Reprinted with permission.

For teams in educational settings to be successful, the culture needs to support faculty and staff involvement. The traditional authority structure of many schools does not support decision making at lower levels, and this can lead to the failure of many teams. Teamwork is an example of lateral decision making as opposed to the traditional vertical decision making that occurs in the organizational hierarchy based on rank or position in the organization.

CASE STUDIES

The following case studies describe leadership situations in educational settings that can be evaluated using the team leadership approach. The first case describes a school improvement team at a middle school.

The second case details a faculty member's efforts to lead a team preparing an accreditation report.

At the end of each case, you will find two sets of questions that will help in analyzing the case. The first set can be answered using information provided in this chapter; the second set, Advanced Questions, provides an opportunity to analyze the case using ideas from the team leadership model and is designed to coincide with the concepts discussed in Chapter 14 of *Leadership: Theory and Practice* (8th ed., pp. 371–402).

SCHOOL IMPROVEMENT
TEAM TROUBLES

Gloria Thorson has taken over as principal of Linden Park Middle School, a public school of nearly 1,000 students in a midsize city. The school has had its share of troubles and was rated as failing by the state's assessment teams. Gloria has been brought on by the superintendent to bring the school up to an appropriate level and keep the state from intervening in its functioning.

Gloria's first undertaking is to establish a School Improvement Team (SIT) comprising teachers, staff, and parents to tackle various aspects of the school's problems from its low literacy rates to its demoralized teachers. While Gloria knows the school needs to work on a host of problems, she decides for the first year to charge the SIT with two goals: establish programs to improve literacy rates and tackle the bullying issues among students.

Both committees are composed of teachers, several parents, and one staff member from the school district office. Gloria meets with each of the committees and clarifies the tasks the groups need to accomplish: (1) research successful middle school literacy and bullying programs, (2) choose a program that has a record of success elsewhere to implement, and then (3) seek external funding to finance the program.

After two months, the SIT reconvenes. It's apparent the Bullying Committee is flourishing. After analyzing data and information provided by school staff members about the bullying situation at Linden Park, the team members have identified a program, #NoBullies, that has been successful in middle schools elsewhere in the state with similar issues and demographics. Two of the teachers and one parent member traveled to two of the schools that are using the #NoBullies program to learn everything they needed to know to implement the program at Linden Park. Another parent found a local foundation willing to provide a grant to fund the program. The committee has prepared a report and has asked to schedule a special SIT meeting with the district's superintendent to present its proposal and get approval for implementation.

Unfortunately, the Literacy Committee's report is not finished. The committee, which includes four of the school's language arts teachers, hasn't made any progress identifying successful programs to model. "Not that there aren't any," says one committee member, "but we are so busy trying to do our own work that we just can't get to it." Gloria asks the committee members what their plan of action is. "Just keep trying to fit it in," says one of the teachers. The parent members of the committee are silent during the meeting. Afterward, Gloria asks one of those parents, Marcus Mead, to stay and talk.

Marcus explains that the committee has not had regular meetings because the members can't find a universally agreeable time. The teachers want to try to meet during their planning time during the day, but several of the parents can't get away from their jobs to do so. Two of the teachers can't meet in the evenings because they have other duties: One's a soccer coach, and the other owns a small business that she runs at night. Marcus says they can work around the meeting issue because they can email and teleconference, but where the committee has gotten stuck is on the work plan. The teachers feel they should be the ones to develop the plan for the group, based on their knowledge and experience of literacy programs, but they haven't been able to do so. Marcus says he's sympathetic to the teachers—they have a lot of work and long days—but that the parent members of the committee are becoming disillusioned and frustrated. Two are talking about quitting.

"We don't want our committee to fail," Marcus says. "It's too important to this school. But we just can't get off square one."

(Continued)

(Continued)

Questions

1. Using the three leadership decisions outlined in the Hill Model for Team Leadership (Figure 14.1), should Gloria

    *   monitor the team or take action,

    *   intervene to meet task or relational needs, or

    *   intervene internally or externally?

2. What internal leadership actions would be needed in this situation?

3. What external leadership actions would be needed?

Advanced Questions

4. How would you describe the two committees in terms of shared or distributed leadership? Give specifics to defend your answer.

5. Do you think the Bullying Committee meets the characteristics of team excellence? Explain your answer.

6. Effective groups have clear norms of conduct. How could you establish norms to improve the Literacy Committee's functioning?

—Authors

CASE 14.2

THE ACCREDITATION TEAM

Christine Winchester is the youngest member of the voice department faculty of Southwestern State University (SSU) and the only one with a PhD. The rest of the voice faculty joined the department when it was formed 30 years ago and came from professional performance backgrounds. At the time the department started, many universities in the rural parts of the American Southwest, where SSU is located, were doing whatever they could to make it appealing for faculty to work so far from urban areas. As a result, many faculty members who did not have advanced degrees were hired, and tenure was often granted automatically.

Because Christine has an advanced degree, the other faculty members treat her with suspicion. They believe their art can only be learned through performance, not in the classroom. As a new faculty member, Christine has all of the same pressures that most new academics face: She must publish, perform professionally, participate on university committees, and raise the university's profile in both the academic and performance circles. At the end of Christine's first year, the department chair, Dr. LeRoy, asks her to lead the committee to renew SSU's accreditation by the National Association of Schools of Music (NASM). Christine is flattered by Dr. LeRoy's faith in her, but concerned about how she is going to lead a committee of other voice faculty when they seem distrustful of her and disrespectful of her work.

The NASM accreditation application is a document made up of many smaller reports that analyze every aspect of the department's functioning from recruitment of students to curriculum. At the committee's first meeting, Christine begins by going over the department's previous successful application from 10 years ago. She has decided that the most efficient way to approach the report is to

(Continued)

(Continued)

have everyone revise the sections he or she wrote 10 years before. She hands out the sections, both in hard copy and on a flash drive; goes over the expectations for the revisions; and sets the next meeting for a month later.

The faculty members reconvene the next month and hand Christine their reports. It is immediately apparent to Christine that none of the committee members even bothered to revise their reports. The dates in the documents have been changed, but everything else is exactly the same as it was in the previous application. Frustrated, Christine dismisses the meeting and goes back to her office feeling defeated. The report has to get done, and at this point doing it herself feels like the easiest course of action, but she knows that isn't practical.

Christine decides that her original plan to assign the reports, collect them, and then edit and assemble the final copies is clearly not going to work. She believes that the task at hand is clearly defined, so there can't be any confusion about what she asked the committee members to do. Christine decides to take another approach and meet with each faculty member individually and go over his or her separate report, getting to know the faculty member and his or her accomplishments better and then suggesting the necessary revisions to the report. The team member will then be asked to revise his or her document and resubmit by a specific deadline. Christine knows this process will take extra time, effort, and patience on her part, but in the end she will have improved her relationships with the faculty.

The process takes most of the year, and when the reports are all edited and the application complete, Christine calls a final meeting. With everyone assembled, Christine thanks and praises the team members for their work, both individually and collectively. The efforts pay off, as Southwestern State University's application is accepted and its membership in NASM renewed for another 10 years.

Questions

1. Based on the Hill Model for Team Leadership (Figure 14.1), what leadership decisions did Christine make when deciding whether to intervene in her team's functioning?

2. Did Christine need to take internal or external leadership actions to get the team to function effectively?

3. Many of Christine's actions are relational. Could she have used more task actions to achieve the team's goals?

Advanced Questions

4. How was shared or distributed leadership used in this situation? Give specifics to defend your answer.

5. Applying conditions of group effectiveness and characteristics of team excellence, would you say Christine's team leadership was successful?

6. What would you suggest Christine have done differently?

—Anne Lape, Educator

REFERENCES

Hill, S. E. K. (2019). Team leadership. In P. G. Northouse (Ed.), *Leadership: Theory and practice* (8th ed., p. 374). Thousand Oaks, CA: SAGE.

Parker, G. M. (1990). *Team players and teamwork*. San Francisco, CA: Jossey-Bass.

15

Gender and Leadership

INTRODUCTION

Education is a field replete with women. Women largely outnumber men as classroom teachers: 73% of U.S. public school teachers are women according to the U.S. Department of Labor (2016). The percentage of female public school principals is 52%, while 55% of private school principals are women (Bitterman, Goldring, & Gray, 2013). But something happens on the way to the administration building. Just 13% of school superintendents are women according to a report by AASA, the School Superintendents Association (Finnan & McCord, 2017).

The numbers are even bleaker in higher education. Women account for only 26% of university presidents, 10% of full professors, and less than 30% of college and university board members (Colorado Women's College, 2013). Women are more likely than men to have entry-level faculty positions—50% of instructors and lecturers are women. This is despite the fact women earn 57% of the bachelor's degrees, 60% of the master's degrees, and more than half of the doctoral degrees in the United States. At the same time, women faculty members earn 20% less than their male colleagues (National Center for Education Statistics, 2011).

Table 15.1 What's Holding Women Back? Barriers Women Encounter on the Leadership Ladder

Human Capital	Gender Differences	Prejudice
1. Amount of Education 2. Amount of Work Experience 3. Fewer Developmental Opportunities 4. Work–Home Conflicts	1. Perceived Ineffective Leadership Styles 2. Perceived Less Commitment and Motivation 3. Less Self-Promotion 4. Less Likely to Negotiate 5. Less Likely to Have Leadership Traits	1. Pervasive Gender Stereotypes 2. Biased Perceptions and Evaluations 3. Vulnerability and Reactance 4. Pressures From Double Standards

SOURCE: Adapted from "Women and Leadership" by Crystal Hoyt in *Leadership Theory and Practice*, 6th ed., by Peter Northouse, 2013.

As explored in *Leadership: Theory and Practice* (8th ed.) in the gender and leadership chapter by Stefanie Simon and Crystal L. Hoyt, these numeric disparities are evidence of a wider leadership gender gap, a global phenomenon whereby women are disproportionately concentrated in lower-level and lower-authority positions. As Simon and Hoyt (2019) explain, there are generally three sets of explanations for the barriers women encounter on their leadership journey, which has been dubbed the *leadership labyrinth* (Table 15.1):

- *human capital*, which encompasses education, training, and work experience as well as work–home conflicts;

- *gender differences* between men and women; and

- *prejudice* based on gender-based stereotypes.

So how does a field that is dominated by women in its lower ranks ultimately reach parity in its top leadership positions? As with other fields and disciplines, it will take significant organizational reform to make this happen—including changes in workplace norms and developmental opportunities for women; greater gender equity in domestic responsibilities; greater negotiation power of women, especially regarding the work–home balance; the effectiveness and predominance of women-owned businesses; and changes in the incongruity between women and leadership.

CASE STUDIES

The following case studies provide practice in diagnosing and making recommendations on situations confronting female leaders in educational settings. The first case describes a school system comptroller who fails to move up in her career despite outstanding performance. The second case examines the difficulties encountered by the first and only female member of a community college's executive team.

At the end of each case, you will find two sets of questions that will help in analyzing the case. The first set can be answered using information provided in this chapter; the second set, Advanced Questions, provides an opportunity to analyze the case using ideas from the concepts discussed in Chapter 15 of *Leadership: Theory and Practice* (8th ed., pp. 403–432).

CASE 15.1

"MY GIRL"

Pat Andrews is the comptroller of the 3,000-student River Valley Community School System. She has been with the public school system for 10 years, having started as a secretary. The first member of her family to go to college, Pat is proud of her achievements and has risen to a level in her career beyond what she dreamed possible.

Pat had been comptroller for five years when Henry Dalton was hired as River Valley's superintendent of schools and became Pat's boss. Henry immediately recognized Pat's work ethic and value to the district. He encouraged Pat to strengthen her skills by engaging in professional development opportunities and earning a master's degree in educational leadership. Henry even took extra time to assist Pat with her classwork and proofread her thesis. When Pat graduated, Henry presented her with a leather-bound copy of her thesis and a pair of pearl earrings. In the card accompanying the gifts, Henry wrote, "I always knew 'My Girl' could do it. Congratulations!"

Despite calling her "My Girl," Pat and Henry's relationship has always been very professional. They do not see one another outside the office, other than the occasional office function, where spouses and families are also present. Pat had expected that once she had a master's degree, a promotion would surely be close behind, either to assistant superintendent of River Valley or as a comptroller for the entire school district. Henry often speaks of looking out for Pat's interests and assisting her in finding a more prestigious position. But a year goes by, and so do a number of opportunities for Pat to advance, and nothing comes of them.

The River Valley Community School System is now preparing to ask the community to vote on a bond issue, and Henry asks the

(Continued)

school board to approve a new position to oversee a campaign explaining the bond issue to the voters and to ensure its passage. Pat is certain that the job will be hers. Instead, Henry brings in Mark Andrews, a former colleague from Henry's previous district. When Pat asks Henry why he didn't consider her, he remarks that he doesn't know what he'd do without "his girl" right where she is, by his side. Henry frequently seeks out Pat's thoughts and suggestions on projects, but Pat has begun to become more aware that she rarely receives credit for her ideas.

Pat's female coworkers see her as a leader, and often come to her for advice. But in staff meetings, when Pat's experience and education give her unique insight into the topic at hand, her male colleagues seem to not acknowledge that she has spoken. In the end, many of the important decisions are made on the golf course after work, or on Fridays at the guys' favorite tap house. None of the women in the office are ever invited to these informal functions.

Pat's master's degree has earned her more responsibility in the office with a slight increase in pay, but it has not brought her the expected promotion. Of the women in her office, Pat holds the highest position of responsibility, but it was a position she held before Henry arrived. During Henry's tenure, the only promotions women have received have been lateral ones (e.g., better secretarial positions). Henry frequently remarks in public that "his gals" are the best around, and do all the "real work" of the district. He praises them often, treats them to lunch, and will leave flowers on their desks. But acknowledgement in the form of pay raises or career advancement is not forthcoming. Pat is grateful to Henry; without his encouragement, she doubts she would have ever pursued her master's degree. But she is bewildered by the lack of respect she now feels from him and wonders what happened to all the promises he had alluded to regarding the future of her career.

Questions

1. Did Pat's relationship with Henry help her career or hold her back? Defend your answer.

2. How is the labyrinth illustrated in Henry's treatment of the women of the River Valley Community School System?

3. How should Pat handle the barriers she is encountering from her male coworkers?

Advanced Questions

4. What career steps would you advise Pat to take? Specifically, how should she approach her relationship with Henry?

5. Could this case be an illustration of what Simon and Hoyt (2019) describe as the "incongruity between the female gender role and the leadership role" (p. 413)? Defend your answer.

6. Describe what type of organizational changes could be made to benefit Pat and other women in her division. Who would need to initiate those changes, and how should they do it?

—Anne Lape, Educator

CASE 15.2

THE EXECUTIVE LEADERSHIP TEAM

The community college had been in operation under the same organizational structure for nearly 50 years: run by the president, Dr. Lloyd Matthews, and the chancellor, Dr. Harry Grossman. The remainder of the college's executive team was composed of five vice presidents, representing programs in business, liberal arts, criminal justice, human services, and information technology (IT).

During the executive team's monthly meeting, Dr. Jorgé Marcos, vice president of information technology, announced his resignation and suggested that the executive team immediately begin a search for his replacement. After advertising the position in trade journals and receiving more than 50 applications, the executive leadership team narrowed the search to three candidates. The first candidate was Dr. Jesse Franks, who had taught IT at the high school level for seven years and as an adjunct for a small community college. Other than teaching, he had no other leadership experience. The second candidate, Dr. Bruce Chandler, had a PhD in IT and science, taught at a small private university where he served as the department chair, and also led the university technology team. The final candidate, Dr. Allyson Lockhart, also had a PhD in IT, was currently a vice president at her university, and had published several articles on technology and education. After interviewing each candidate, Dr. Lockhart was selected as the community college's new vice president of information technology.

At first, Dr. Lockhart appeared to be doing well in her new position and had the support of the faculty and the executive leadership team. After about six weeks, however, the faculty in the IT division began to challenge her. Her vision and ideas for increasing enrollment and improving the division were met with negative comments like "Dr. Marcos didn't do it this way" and "What are you trying to prove?" Some faculty resented having a woman in charge, because as they put it "IT is a man's world." Several faculty members also made comments suggesting that she had only been hired "to add some diversity to the leadership team."

Feeling the resistance to her leadership, Dr. Lockhart arranged a meeting with President Matthews to discuss these tensions. She explained that it was becoming difficult to move the division forward because of the highly negative perceptions faculty were expressing about her abilities. This discussion did not yield the results Dr. Lockhart had hoped. Instead, all Dr. Matthews said was that Dr. Lockhart's concerns would be discussed at the next executive leadership team meeting. Until then, he advised her to just take care of the day-to-day issues and not try to make any changes within her division.

When the full executive team met two weeks later, President Matthews ran the meeting, and Dr. Lockhart's concerns were not on the agenda. As the meeting was about to adjourn, she reminded President Matthews of their earlier conversation, noting it was really important to her to receive feedback from the executive team about the faculty concerns within her division. Reluctantly, Dr. Matthews brought up Dr. Lockhart's concerns. But as he did so, he stated, "I appreciate your concerns, Dr. Lockhart, but I think you need to toughen up and lead like a man. It's the only way you'll get more respect." The other male team members chuckled, and some made comments comparing her leadership to that of her predecessor, Dr. Marcos. Feeling like the meeting was not going in a positive direction, Dr. Lockhart left.

After the meeting, she decided to give the situation another month to see if the environment would be more receptive. But at the end of that month, the behavior of the faculty had not improved; if anything, it was worse. The only support Dr. Lockhart received was from the two female faculty in her division. From them, she learned the college's board of trustees was composed entirely of men, that she was the first woman to be promoted to a leadership position at the college, and that she probably was only hired to make the college look good. Armed with this information, Dr. Lockhart requested a meeting with the president, the executive leadership team, and the board of trustees. This request irritated the president, so he called a special executive leadership team meeting. During the

(Continued)

meeting, Dr. Lockhart brought forth the following points: There was no faculty support for her ideas to enhance the program and increase enrollment, her colleagues did not listen to her or include her in decision making, both the faculty and her colleagues constantly compared her leadership to that of her predecessor, and she was perceived by the faculty as the token female.

The team made light of her concerns, including Dr. Matthews, who stated, "Dr. Lockhart, we hired you because we thought you could fit into our culture. It is time you start to play ball with the rest of the team. Even if you were hired to add diversity to the team, you are expected to do what it takes to be successful.

"There are plenty of men whom we could have hired, but we selected you. If women did not expect to be treated delicately, we wouldn't be in this meeting today. Men are tough and ignore what people say. Women need to lead like men, so stop being so sensitive and just get it done."

He concluded by asking, "Do you understand what is expected of you?"

Dr. Lockhart left the meeting with a sick feeling. She had signed a three-year contract and knew leaving this job before the contract was up would be financially disastrous for her.

Questions

1. What barriers of inclusion did Dr. Lockhart face?

2. What does the case suggest about Dr. Lockhart's leadership style compared to Dr. Marcos's?

3. Has Dr. Matthews's leadership been helpful or harmful to Dr. Lockhart? Explain your answer.

Advanced Questions

4. How does this case illustrate gender differences in leadership? Are these real or perceived differences? Give examples to explain your answer.

5. What organizational changes need to be made to benefit Dr. Lockhart and other women who may follow her? Who needs to initiate those changes, and how should he or she go about doing it?

6. What can Dr. Lockhart do on her own to become an accepted leader and a member of the organization?

—Joanne Barnes, Indiana Wesleyan University

REFERENCES

Bitterman, A., Goldring, R., & Gray, L. (2013). *Characteristics of public and private elementary and secondary school principals in the United States: Results from the 2011–12 schools and staffing survey* (NCES 2013-313). Washington, DC: U.S. Department of Education, National Center for Education Statistics. Retrieved from http://nces.ed.gov/pubsearch

Colorado Women's College. (2013). *Benchmarking women's leadership in the United States 2013.* Denver, CO: Author.

Finnan, L. A., & McCord, R. S. (2017, February). *2016 AASA Superintendent Salary & Benefits Study.* Alexandria, VA: AASA, the School Superintendents Association. Retrieved from http://www.aasa.org/research.aspx

Hoyt, C. (2013). Women and leadership. In P. G. Northouse (Ed.), *Leadership: Theory and practice* (6th ed., pp. 349–382). Thousand Oaks, CA: SAGE.

Kowalski, T. J., McCord, R. S., Petersen, G. J., Young, I. P., & Ellerson, N. M. (2011). *American school superintendent: 2010 decennial study.* Lanham, MD: Rowman & Littlefield Education.

National Center for Education Statistics. (2011). *Digest of education statistics* [Bachelor's, master's, and doctor's degrees conferred by degree-granting institutions, by sex of student and discipline division: 2010–11, Table 317]. Retrieved from http://nces.ed.gov/programs/digest/d12/tables/dt12_317.asp

Simon, S., & Hoyt, C. L. (2019). Gender and leadership. In P. G. Northouse (Ed.), *Leadership: Theory and practice* (8th ed., pp. 403–431). Thousand Oaks, CA: Sage.

U.S. Department of Labor (2016). *Labor force statistics from the Current Population Survey.* Bureau of Labor Market Statistics. Retrieved from https://www.bls.gov/cps/cpsaat11.htm

16

Culture and Leadership

There's no doubt that globalization has changed the world of education. Not only are more and more of our students coming from international backgrounds, requiring educational leaders to become competent in cross-cultural awareness and practice, but globalization requires that those we teach understand cultural differences as well.

In *Leadership: Theory and Practice* (8th ed.), *culture* is defined as the learned beliefs, values, rules, norms, symbols, and traditions that are common to a group of people. It is these *shared* qualities of a group that make it unique. Culture is dynamic and transmitted to others. In short, culture is the way of life, customs, and script of a group of people (Gudykunst & Ting-Toomey, 1988).

Related to culture are the terms *multicultural* and *diversity*. *Multicultural* implies an approach or a system that takes more than one culture into account. It refers to the existence of multiple cultures such as African, American, Asian, European, and Middle Eastern. *Multicultural* can also refer to a set of subcultures defined by race, gender, ethnicity, sexual orientation, or age. *Diversity* refers to the existence of different cultures or ethnicities within a group or an organization.

Adler and Bartholomew (1992, p. 53) contended that leaders need to develop five cross-cultural competencies:

1. Leaders need to understand business, political, and cultural environments worldwide.

2. Leaders need to learn the perspectives, tastes, trends, and technologies of many other cultures.

3. Leaders need to be able to work simultaneously with people from many cultures.

4. Leaders must be able to adapt to living and communicating in other cultures.

5. Leaders need to learn to relate to people from other cultures from a position of equality rather than cultural superiority.

Two factors that can inhibit cultural awareness are *ethnocentrism* and *prejudice*. Ethnocentrism is the human tendency to place one's own group at the center of one's observations of others and the world. It is problematic for leaders because it prevents them from fully understanding the world of others. Similarly, prejudice consists of judgments about others based on fixed attitudes and unsubstantiated data. Prejudice has a negative impact because it is self-oriented and inhibits leaders from seeing the many facets and qualities of others.

In the past 30 years, many studies have focused on identifying various dimensions of culture. The best known of these is the work of Hofstede (1980, 2001), who identified five major dimensions: power distance, uncertainty avoidance, individualism–collectivism, masculinity–femininity, and long-term–short-term orientation. Expanding on Hofstede's work, House, Hanges, Javidan, Dorfman, and Gupta (2004) delineated additional dimensions of culture, including in-group collectivism, institutional collectivism, future orientation, assertiveness, performance orientation, and humane orientation.

Table 16.1 Universally Desirable Leadership Attributes

Positive Leader Attributes

Trustworthy	Just	Honest
Has foresight	Plans ahead	Encouraging
Positive	Dynamic	Motive arouser
Confidence builder	Motivational	Dependable
Intelligent	Decisive	Effective bargainer
Win-win problem solver	Communicative	Informed
Administratively skilled	Coordinative	Team builder
Excellence oriented		

SOURCE: Adapted from House, R. J., Hanges, P. J., Javidan, M., Dorfman, P. W., & Gupta, V. (Eds.). (2004). *Culture, Leadership, and Organizations: The GLOBE Study of 62 Societies.* Thousand Oaks, CA: SAGE.

By far, however, the Global Leadership and Organizational Behavior Effectiveness, or GLOBE, studies offer the strongest body of findings to date on culture and leadership. Using quantitative research methods, GLOBE researchers studied how 17,000 managers from 62 different countries viewed leadership. They analyzed the similarities and differences between regional clusters of cultural groups by grouping countries into 10 distinct clusters: Anglo, Latin Europe, Nordic Europe, Germanic Europe, Eastern Europe, Latin America, the Middle East, Sub-Saharan Africa, Southern Asia, and Confucian Asia.

One outcome of the GLOBE project was the identification of a list of universally endorsed positive and negative attributes of leadership. An exceptional leader has a high degree of integrity, charisma, and interpersonal skill (Table 16.1). An ineffective leader is someone who is asocial, malevolent, self-focused, and autocratic (Table 16.2).

Without a doubt, leaders inside and outside the classroom are faced with dilemmas every day that are a result of cultural differences. Understanding the dynamics of another culture and how the culture views leadership can help us all function better in an increasingly multicultural world.

Table 16.2 Universally Undesirable Leadership Attributes

Negative Leader Attributes

Loner	Asocial	Noncooperative
Irritable	Nonexplicit	Egocentric
Ruthless	Dictatorial	

SOURCE: Adapted from House, R. J., Hanges, P. J., Javidan, M., Dorfman, P. W., & Gupta, V. (Eds.). (2004). *Culture, Leadership, and Organizations: The GLOBE Study of 62 Societies.* Thousand Oaks, CA: SAGE.

CASE STUDIES

The following case studies provide examples of cultural contexts in educational settings. The first case describes a new Caucasian school principal at a school with a high minority student population. The second case examines implementation of an international student program at a university in the Midwest.

At the end of each case, you will find two sets of questions that will help in analyzing the case. The first set can be answered using information provided in this chapter; the second set, Advanced Questions, provides an opportunity to analyze the case using the concepts about culture and leadership that are discussed in Chapter 16 of *Leadership: Theory and Practice* (8th ed., pp. 433–472).

CASE 16.1

EMPTY PLAYGROUND

Mary Perkins is the new principal of the 250-student Lake Street Elementary, a public school for Grades pre-K–5 located in an urban neighborhood. Lake Street's student population is 65% African American, 25% Hispanic, and 10% Caucasian. Mary took the principal's position after working for a number of years as principal at an elementary school in the small, rural town she grew up in. Even though the student population at the last elementary school she worked for was primarily Caucasian, Mary is not concerned about her ability to adapt to the diversity of her new school because she believes all children are alike at heart.

One of Mary's first tasks as Lake Street's principal is to renovate the school's playground. The playground consists of metal swings, slides, and a merry-go-round on a hard grass surface. Mary ordered new, modern equipment, and arranged to have the playground's grass surface dug out and filled with sand. As fall arrives, Mary is thrilled with the finished playground and looks forward to seeing children playing on beautiful new slides and swings.

School opens, and the students arrive, dressed up for the first day of school. The halls are filled with parents taking photos, cheerful hellos, and tearful goodbyes. The playground doesn't see much use the first day of school, but Mary doesn't think much of it. As the week goes by, however, Mary notices that the new playground equipment isn't getting much use by the children at all. She starts spending lunch recess outside with the children, and every day the pattern is the same. The children playing on the playground are predominantly the white children and a few of the Hispanic children. The African American children keep to the sidewalks, a few with basketballs or jump ropes, but most just stand around until recess is over. In the classrooms, however, Mary observes that the children intermingle and are friendly with one another. They partner up during PE and art class. None of the teachers report any major cases of bullying in the classrooms, so Mary dismisses the idea that the separation on the playground is a racial issue. But something isn't right.

A few weeks later, Mary is watching the children playing at recess, sadly noting the same children aren't using the playground, when she is approached by Destiny Johnson, an African American parent who has volunteered for recess duty.

"It's a shame not all the kids can use the new playground," Destiny says.

"What do you mean?" Mary asks. "The playground is open to every child."

"Haven't you noticed that the Black kids won't go near it? It's because their moms have told them not to," Destiny says.

Mary is stunned. "Why would their moms tell them not to play on the new playground?"

"It's the sand," explains Destiny. "With the oil we put in our kids' hair and the twists and braids they have, if they get sand in their hair, it will take us all day to get it out. So we've told our kids to find somewhere else to play during recess."

Mary is terribly embarrassed. Her ignorance has effectively banned the majority of her students from their own playground. "I am so sorry—I had no idea," she says.

Destiny nods. "I didn't think so," she says. "I told the other moms that, but they feel like you really didn't care if the Black kids could use it or not."

At the next monthly meeting of the Parent Association, Mary begins the meeting by apologizing for her mistake, and then asks parents to offer some alternative playground surfaces that will be acceptable to all children. In the end, one father, who works for a landscaping firm, offers to replace the sand with wood mulch, getting the mulch at cost from his employer. By the end of the month, the Lake Street playground is filled with children.

(Continued)

(Continued)

Questions

1. How did Mary's ethnocentrism hinder her leadership of Lake Street Elementary?

2. What could Mary have done to be more prepared to be the leader of a new student population?

3. In Mary's solution to the problem, what universal leadership attributes did she demonstrate?

Advanced Questions

4. In addition to keeping some students from being able to use the playground, what other consequences did the new playground have for Mary?

5. How might Mary's lack of awareness about the cultures of her students be a problem for her in the future? What leadership actions can she take to prevent that?

6. Do you think the parents should have approached her as soon as they realized there was a problem? Why do you think they didn't?

— Anne Lape, Educator

CASE 16.2

WELCOME TO THE HEARTLAND

WorldEd is a for-profit corporation that recruits students to attend partnership universities throughout the world. Unlike other for-profit higher education student recruiting agencies, WorldEd provides pathways to higher education for a less-select group of international students who, despite their respectable academic performance in high school, find gaining acceptance into a foreign university very challenging if not impossible. Higher-performing students from foreign countries are sought after and have no problems attending the universities of their choice.

International students who want to come to the United States to study often pick California as their state of choice, due to its diverse population. As a result, California's universities are highly selective of the students they admit. WorldEd sees the need to expand into less expensive, high-quality universities in other regions of the United States. WorldEd has decided to expand its market into the Midwest, which has many quality universities at very affordable tuition rates. Additionally, the cost of living in much of the region is approximately half of the expense found in California.

After extensive research and negotiations, WorldEd has estab-lished a partnership with the University of the Heartland. The University of the Heartland is a public university located in a very conservative region, and while the people are friendly and outgo-ing, their conservative values could create challenges for a group of diverse people trying to assimilate into their community. WorldEd feels it can handle that challenge as it has previous expe-rience in assimilating international students into a conservative university in Chile. Although that conservative university is in a different culture, WorldEd is confident that the model used in Chile

(Continued)

(Continued)

will succeed at the University of the Heartland. The key, from WorldEd's experience, is to provide the university and local community frequent and continuous awareness of the international students along with providing education to faculty, staff, and students regarding cultural differences.

The first cohort of 150 international students arrives at the University of the Heartland for the fall semester. This group consists of undergraduate and graduate students from Egypt, Turkey, Qatar, Malaysia, India, Brazil, Japan, China, Taiwan, Nigeria, and Zambia. WorldEd modified the Chile assimilation model to accommodate the U.S. culture and is sure that its international students will encounter few if any issues. Initially, the assimilation plan works well, and students are received warmly. However, as the semester progresses, issues start to surface within the university and community as well as among the international students.

Professors are becoming frustrated with several groups of international students. They report that the students from Egypt, Turkey, and Qatar generally seem to lack a sense of prior planning and time management. The Chinese and Taiwanese students are extremely shy and lack critical thinking skills, although the professors admit that it is difficult to determine this due to the students' lack of participation in class. The students from Brazil are a very close-knit group, unwilling to venture beyond their small group. International students from many countries are having problems integrating and cooperating with each other both in and out of class.

Community members are also becoming upset with the international students, especially the landlords who rent apartments to the students. There are complaints that some of the international students do not maintain appropriate health and cleanliness standards in their apartments and are rude to the female managers. Other community members are having a difficult time accepting the differing religious beliefs of the international students as the local community is predominantly Christian.

While some see the initial year of the WorldEd program at the University of the Heartland to be a limited success, the program's director feels changes need to be made to help with the assimilation issues. Not only does the orientation program for incoming WorldEd students need to be adjusted, but the director also sees a need for continuing education for the faculty and local community.

Questions

1. How are the community's and faculty's reactions examples of ethnocentrism and prejudice? Give examples.

2. If you were the director, what would be some ways you could educate the faculty and community about cultural differences?

3. Why do you think the model from Chile that WorldEd was using didn't work as well for the students attending the University of the Heartland?

Advanced Questions

4. Use the GLOBE research to identify the different cultural clusters represented in the initial international student cohort. How are these cultural clusters different?

5. Which dimension of culture poses the greatest challenge for each international student cultural cluster when assimilating into the University of the Heartland culture?

6. How can the director of WorldEd use the leadership profiles of each cultural cluster to better assimilate the international students into the university and local culture?

7. Which group of international students should WorldEd anticipate having the most difficult time assimilating into the university student body, and why?

—*John Baker, Western Kentucky University*

REFERENCES

Adler, N. J., & Bartholomew, S. (1992). Managing globally competent people. *Academy of Management Executive, 6,* 52–65.

Gudykunst, W. B., & Ting-Toomey, S. (1988). *Culture and interpersonal communication.* Newbury Park, CA: SAGE.

Hofstede, G. (1980). *Culture's consequences: International differences in work-related values.* Beverly Hills, CA: SAGE.

Hofstede, G. (2001). *Culture's consequences: Comparing values, behaviors, institutions, and organizations across nations.* Thousand Oaks, CA: SAGE.

House, R. J., Hanges, P. J., Javidan, M., Dorfman, P. W., & Gupta, V. (Eds.). (2004). *Culture, leadership, and organizations: The GLOBE study of 62 societies.* Thousand Oaks, CA: SAGE.

Index

About the Authors

Peter G. Northouse is a professor emeritus of communication in the School of Communication at Western Michigan University. For more than 25 years he taught leadership and interpersonal and organizational communication at both the undergraduate and graduate levels. In addition to publications in professional journals he is the author of *Leadership: Theory and Practice* (8th ed.) and *Introduction to Leadership: Concepts and Practice* (4th ed.) and co-author of *Health Communication: Strategies for Health Professionals* (3rd ed.). His scholarly and curricular interests include models of leadership, leadership assessment, ethical leadership, and leadership and group dynamics. He has worked as a consultant in a variety of areas, including leadership development, leadership education, conflict management, and health communication. He holds a doctorate in speech communication from the University of Denver and master's and bachelor's degrees in communication education from Michigan State University.

Marie Lee is an editor and educator who has taught communication courses at Western Michigan University and as a consultant. With a background in journalism, she has written numerous articles and edited books, including Northouse's *Leadership: Theory and Practice* (8th ed.) and *Introduction to Leadership: Concepts and Practice* (4th ed.). She is co-owner and editor of Encore Publications Inc., a publishing company in Kalamazoo, Michigan. She has a master's degree in organizational communication from Western Michigan University and a bachelor's degree in journalism from Idaho State University.

About the Contributors

John Baker is an associate professor of organizational leadership at Western Kentucky University, an academic unit in the School of Professional Studies, University College. Prior to joining WKU in 2006, Baker had a career in the U.S. Army where he spent more than 26 years on active duty serving throughout the United States and overseas. Baker's research interests focus on peer and military leadership. Baker has an EdD in educational leadership from Western Kentucky University as well as master's degrees in physical geography from the University of Wisconsin and engineering management from Drexel University.

Joanne Barnes is the dean of the Graduate School and a professor of organizational leadership in graduate studies at Indiana Wesleyan University, and has been involved in higher education since 1996. In 2008, Barnes retired from Delphi Electronics & Safety in Kokomo, Indiana, after nearly 37 years of service, where she held various management and leadership positions, including global quality systems manager where she was responsible for implementing global change and driving common quality practices throughout Europe, Asia, North America, and South America and for leading global teams. Her current research involves cultural intelligence, multicultural leadership, and the cross-transferability of Western-based theories and assessments to Eastern European and Asian cultures. She has presented at several top conferences on leadership and has publications on women and leadership, cultural intelligence, and global leadership to name a few. Barnes is a certified trainer/coach in the Intercultural Effectiveness

Scale, the Global Competencies Inventory, and Cultural Intelligence. Barnes earned an EdD in organizational leadership from Indiana Wesleyan University.

Trevor J. Davies is a senior program associate with the David P. Weikart Center for Youth Program Quality, a division of the Forum for Youth Investment. His work includes providing coaching, training, and consultation services to the Weikart Center's clients, including Michigan's 21st Century Community Learning Centers and the *Technical Assistance and Coaching Support Systems* initiative. Davies's graduate studies and field experiences continue to shape the Weikart Center's coaching methodology, including the development of the *Coaching for Continuous Improvement* training program. He has a master's degree in communication from Western Michigan University.

Anne Lape has been a teacher for 20 years, teaching every grade from pre-K through 12 in private, public, urban, suburban, rural, and home school settings. As a middle school teacher in 2010, she sent more students to the national level of the National History Day competition than any other teacher in Michigan. Lape is a two-time fellow and teacher consultant for the National Writing Project whose own poetry has been published in *Home and Other Places*. She is a successful grant writer and presented on educational topics at state and national conferences.

David Rosch is an associate professor in the agricultural education program at the University of Illinois at Urbana-Champaign. His areas of interest include college student leadership development and the effects of leadership programs and courses on development. He has worked at the University of Illinois since 2006, beginning at the Illinois Leadership Center and becoming faculty in the agricultural education program in 2011. He currently teaches leadership theory and methods courses and conducts research in emerging adult leadership development. He has served in a variety of capacities in the International Leadership Association and the Association of Leadership Educators, has served as a co–lead facilitator for LeaderShape and co-chair of the National Leadership Symposium, and is currently the curriculum chair for the

Leadership Education Academy. Rosch has a PhD in higher postsecondary education from Syracuse University, a master's degree from Colorado State University, and a bachelor's degree in psychology and sociology from Binghamton University.

Thomas Starmack earned his EdD at the University of Pittsburgh. He is a professor of education at Bloomsburg University, where he coordinates the graduate program in educational leadership. He conducts regional professional development for school and district-level administrators and consults for various pre-K–12 school districts in central Pennsylvania. Starmack is a former secondary mathematics teacher, pre-K–12 school principal, and assistant superintendent. He was the recipient of the 2001 Milken Family Foundation Educator Award and the 2010 Pennsylvania ASCD Supervision and Curriculum Development Award.

Christopher W. Tremblay is a research and marketing consultant for Michigan State University's Gifted and Talented Education and also serves as director of AACRAO's Strategic Enrollment Management (SEM) Endorsement Program. He has held various enrollment management positions at the University of Wisconsin–Superior, Western Michigan University, University of Michigan–Dearborn, and Gannon University. Tremblay earned both his bachelor's and master's degrees from Western Michigan University. He has a post-master's certificate in enrollment management from Capella University and an EdD in educational leadership from the University of Michigan–Dearborn. He has presented at 75 association conferences nationally and internationally. He has published articles in four journals: *College & University*, *The Journal of College Admission*, *Journal of College Orientation and Transition*, and *The Journal of Intergroup Relations*. Tremblay serves as co-editor of the *Journal of College Access* and is the author of the book, *Walt's Pilgrimage*, a travel guide on the life of Walt Disney.